War and Democracy

Paul Gottfried

War
and
Democracy

Selected Essays 1975–2012

ARKTOS
LONDON 2012

First edition published in 2012 by Arktos Media Ltd.

Copyright © 2012 by Arktos Media Ltd.

Printed in the United Kingdom.

ISBN 978-1-907166-80-8

BIC classification:
Conservatism and right-of-centre democratic ideologies (JPFM)
Social & political philosophy (HPS)
General and world history (HBG)

Editor: Tobias Ridderstråle
Cover Design & Layout: Daniel Friberg

Cover image: An American soldier on patrol in Iraq in front of
a poster showing Muslim cleric and politician Sadeq al-Sadr.
Photograph by Petros Giannakouris/AP/PA.

ARKTOS MEDIA LTD
www.arktos.com

TABLE OF CONTENTS

INTRODUCTION

The decision of Arktos Media to publish this anthology of essays has led me into reflecting on the major changes in my political thinking over the last forty years. Strangely enough, the ideas I held forty years ago as an interpreter of contemporary history are much closer to the ones I now hold than to those I adopted in the intervening years. In my writings into the mid-1970s one finds a preoccupation with cultural decadence, as reflected in the work of nineteenth- and early twentieth-century European thinkers. Schopenhauer, Nietzsche, Spengler, the Swiss historian Jacob Burckhardt, and late nineteenth-century French literature were all subjects I treated sympathetically in this time period, together with the anti-modernist critique of the Southern Agrarians. I was also struck as a graduate student at Yale and then, as an assistant professor at Case-Western Reserve in Cleveland by the millenarian scheme that seem hard-wired into modern Western man and which extended from Christianity down to modern leftist ideologies. There seemed to be a predisposition in our society toward a vision of a perfected humanity or of an end to history. Moreover, in trying to grasp its character, I was impressed more by Nietzsche's comments on slave morality and by Mircea Eliade's analysis of the vision of the triumphant suffering just than by other interpretations of the apocalyptic temptation.

In graduate school I studied the German-American philosopher of history Eric Voegelin, who wrote on the "gnostic" character of the millenarian mind, but unlike this hero of post-war American conservatives, I was skeptical about the explanation given for what I was observing. I never really accepted Voegelin's view that our predisposition toward utopian thinking arose from a recurrent Christian heresy. This mindset seemed more basic to Christian civilization than Voegelin

was willing to recognize, and for reasons at least partly explained by
Nietzsche and Eliade, we were becoming powerless before leftist adap-
tations of a vision that had grown out of the fabric of Western culture. Needless to say, I did not take this modern problem lightly. It has
always seemed to me that much of what is best in our civilization is
tied to our religious heritage, and our inability to deal effectively any
longer with even the most bizarre forms of the egalitarian temptation,
and its accompanying utopian vision, is for me depressing, especially
given the inextricable connection between what is meritorious and
what is distressing in our Western religious heritage. We may now be
left with the problems of this heritage more than with its metaphysi-
cal and ethical benefits. These were my thoughts in the 1970s, which
surfaced again later, and which were most clearly evident in my books
Multiculturalism and the Politics of Guilt (2002) and *The Strange Death
of Marxism* (2005).

A second theme, evidence of which I see in my early writing but
which becomes especially important in my work over the last ten
years, is the raising of current fashionable political values and stands
to timeless truths. Like the millenarian vision that accompanies our
politics, this present-centeredness revolves around escalating stages
of an egalitarian fixation. The denial of genetically rooted differences
among groups, the exaltation of "lifestyles" once deemed as deviant
but now associated with Eliade's "suffering just," and the obliteration of
gender roles as belonging to an oppressive hierarchy that existed in the
prejudiced past, are all characteristic of this *Zeitgeist*. It spills over into
our historical interpretations and renders it impossible to view earlier
ages without taking into account the current order of victims. Indeed,
any deviation in the past from this imposed model of preferred victims and the required sensitivities for approaching them is considered
proof positive of inexcusably reactionary attitudes.

This emphasis on past victims who need to be elevated to special
status is reflected in our talk about "human rights" and "values." What
increasingly pervades such pliable concepts is a focus on universal
equality, an ideal that can only be implemented through a dictatorship
of the righteous. In the U.S. and elsewhere in the Western world, this
project takes the leftist form of a rigorously enforced political correctness, often going under the moniker of anti-fascism or anti-racism.
On the bogus right (as opposed to any genuine counterrevolutionary
force) this egalitarian project takes the even more aggressive form of

an "American global democratic mission." It is seen as the duty of the American superpower and its "allies" to bring women's rights and other blessings of the present American regime to less advanced societies. This mission has been anchored in either made-to-wear "American values" or some modernizing mission that the U.S. is obliged to assume for humanitarian reasons — or because "liberal democracy" is nowhere safe unless it has been universally imposed.

In my middle period, one finds different emphases, particularly in my occasional writings of the 1980s. This is present even in a transitional work leading to my later return to my beginnings, *The Search for Historical Meaning* (1987). In this work, I stress the dialectical historical patterns that affected the fathers of the post-war conservative movement and which I trace back to the often undisclosed influence of the German philosopher Hegel. I try to examine Hegel's effects on the thought of political thinkers and journalists identified with American conservatism (or what there was of it) who rose to fame in the 1950s and 1960s. Like Hegel's view of the German Protestant constitutional monarchy of the early nineteenth century, the U.S. in its origin was viewed by these thinkers as representing a synthesis of order and liberty.

This synthesis had come about through a long, tortuous process stretching back into the ancient world and could only be understood through an experienced past. It was the mistake of the current establishment Right, I explain, to treat the U.S. as a "propositional nation" rather than as the product of a specific Euro-American context, which was endangered by appeals to "abstract universals." My book rails against the human rights ideology that was then taking hold on the right as well as on the left. What began as a celebration of America's beginning and the attempt to locate it in something like Hegel's "concrete universal" ended as a "Conservative Farewell to History." In the final chapter, as the social theorist Robert Nisbet noted in a perceptive review for *National Review* (May 22, 1987) I was bidding farewell to a derailed American Right. But even more significantly I was turning my back on a vision of the American present that I had held for the preceding ten years.

I had vigorously supported the presidential bid of Ronald Reagan in 1980, with the candidate's invocation of American patriotism. In fact I then served as an alternate delegate for Reagan's nomination from the state of Illinois. (Fortunately I was not required to attend that convention because the regular delegate was on hand.) As late as the early 1980s I had faithfully read from cover to cover the neoconservative monthly *Commentary*; and despite my longtime reservations about the global democratic tropes and left-wing imperialism of this movement, I had been impressed by the neoconservatives' steadfast opposition to Communist tyranny. At that time it took courage in the academic and journalistic world to dissent from the pro-Communist or anti-anti-Communist sentiments that one encountered daily in one's professional life; and for whatever reason they were led to assuming this stance, the neoconservatives seemed sound on this point.

Even after the rupture in my relations with this group, a development discussed in detail in my autobiographical *Encounters*, I continued to believe in the American "conservative movement," as the bearer and protector of a sound American political tradition. It was only when I noticed how easily the neoconservatives took over that movement and imposed on it what were essentially leftist revolutionary ideas that it became apparent how little there was to co-opt. Equally important, I began to figure out that there was no critical distinction between what the neoconservatives glorified as "American values" and what their followers understood by them. Welfare state democracy plus a foreign policy akin to what the French Jacobins had advocated in their zeal to bring the "rights of man" everywhere is exactly how *soi-disant* American conservatives understand their tradition. And the content of these rights would expand as they became identified with new progressive agendas, including women's rights and greater acceptance of gay expressive freedoms.

Although I was not opposed to the existence of a Jewish state in the Middle East, it also became annoying how thoroughly the conservative movement and the Republican Party, to which it was joined at the hip, became predictable vehicles for a certain Zionist view. I am certainly not saying that conservatives should not be entitled to take any position they want on Arab-Israeli disputes. The problem is that a very zealous Zionism became foundational for American conservatism with the neoconservative takeover of the movement; and almost any leftist position is now forgivable in the conservative press as long as the politician or journalist in question is "sound on Israel." Later support for Middle Eastern wars, which neoconservatives were instrumental in getting off the ground, has provided a further litmus test for political acceptability by the neoconservative-controlled Right.

This may serve as a lead-in to those opinions and interpretations that my readers will discover in my work since the 1990s. First off, I have become more skeptical about the use of American power than I was during the height of the Cold War. I have also grown critical of "value talk," which in the context of American politics means placing a rhetorical veil over one's political intentions. I no longer find a critical difference between the American Right and the American Left; and except for a certain disparity in power and economic resources, I believe the U.S. is moving along the same trajectory as Western and Central Europe, away from a bourgeois or older Western civilization, toward some form of post-Christian, postmodern culture presided over by a vast administrative apparatus.

Rather than being a counterweight to this trend, the U.S. has abetted it both culturally and politically. Whether through the export of our cultural industry or through our political opposition to anything resembling a nationalist or rightist alternative to Western Europe's politically correct, anti-fascist governments, we have had a huge hand in what has gone on across the Atlantic. This can be seen from our "re-education" of the post-war Germans down to the expressions of comfort among our journalists across the permissible political spectrum with a morally decaying, "progressive" Europe, based on international agencies and something vaguely resembling the "free market." It is a Europe of satellites that we have tried to create, one lacking national traditions and any identity distinct from our made-in-America homogenizing ideology. This fits perfectly into what neoconservative publicist Francis Fukuyama celebrated in the 1990s as the liberal democratic "end of history" under the American aegis. Although pulled along by the same forces, American political elites are delighted by the powerlessness and servility of the Old World. The best they can offer as a remedy to the flood of often hostile Muslims settling in European countries is a campaign to teach the incoming population "human rights" and feminist values.

Western European and German elites are also to blame for this disintegration, and particularly when they complain that we haven't done as much as they have to enforce political correctness and to overthrow traditional social relations. These righteous attacks on Americans, from across the Atlantic and from north of the Canadian border, for not drinking deeply enough of the poisons we have helped release verges on lunacy. It is also a civilizational problem that I think other countries are now aggravating by how they are turning against their political, cultural, and ethical traditions. Their self-important strutting as they sink into chaos and irrelevance illustrates perfectly the ancient aphorism: *Quem Deus vult perdere prius dementat.*[1]

---

1   "Those whom God wishes to destroy, He first makes mad."-Ed.

1. HISTORY OR HYSTERIA

The American Spectator, January 1975

The Failure of Illiberalism:
Essays on the Political Culture of Modern Germany
by Fritz Stern
Knopf 1972, 233 pages

Since the 1930s, the study of German history in America has been dominated by a number of historians whose shared assumptions have not yet been critically examined. The scholars I refer to are the German refugee historians, who have dominated this field, first directly, and then, more recently, through their students. However divided they were on some issues, these personalities brought to their work a distinctive set of prejudices. In fact, this collection of essays by Fritz Stern testifies to the durability of their attitudes. Inasmuch as most of the group — for example, Hans Kohn, Hajo Holborn, Franz Neumann, Georg Mosse and George Lichtheim — were themselves victims of Nazi oppression, it was only natural that they should consider the Hitlerian epoch a focal point for their historical research. All of them were passionately critical of German social traditions, revealing not only the depth of their despair over Nazism but also an iconoclastic spirit often related to their feelings about pre-Hitlerian Germany. They sought to explain the rise and success of Hitler in terms of a culture that was peculiarly German. They attempted to make the past serviceable, as a warning to the world of how their own people had strayed and later as a means for impressing on the Germans the terrible burden of their heritage.

Nonetheless, in my opinion, the pursuit of such tasks led these prophets of wrath into error. It caused them to create hobgoblins out of past figures and movements, which they ultimately placed in some ascending order of culpability for the presence of the Nazi regime. It also tempted them to link the rise of fascism with the failure of their own personal values to win broad acceptance among the German nation. I believe that one can illustrate the effect of these pitfalls by analyzing *The Failure of Illiberalism*, the work of a leading apologist for the type of thought described.

It should be conceded that Stern presents some defensible and occasionally stimulating opinions. His essay on the relationship of Otto von Bismarck, the Prussian nobleman who unified Germany, and Gerson Bleichröder, the Jewish banker who helped subsidize the enterprise, is one case in point. Stern shows considerable psychological insight in discussing the growth of an implausible, but intimate friendship between two figures separated by a veritable social abyss. Elsewhere he offers some interesting, though hardly startling, comments on present-day Germany, East and West, and a fine study of the defects of the Weimar Republic.

Having made these acknowledgements, we may proceed to examine the weaknesses of his presentation. His introduction, which fails in its attempt at imposing thematic unity on the volume, tries to explain the two central catastrophes in modern German history, World War I and its aftermath and the Nazi seizure of power. Stern connects both these watersheds to a certain moral corrosion which supposedly pervaded German society, at least since the formation of the Empire: "illiberalism," a convenient rubric to cover all of the alleged flaws of German national character noted by Teutonophobes since the turn of the century and by many German *émigrés* since 1933. Although the list of abuses contains no surprises, it does make one nostalgic for the simplicities of wartime movies. The Germans, at least for the period between 1870 and 1945, supposedly lacked individuality, were the products of authoritarian households, and believed implicitly in their national superiority. Rising later than most other European powers to a position of political eminence, they suffered from a collective insecurity (Stern prefers the term *Angst*), which caused them to be stridently aggressive in dealing with other peoples. Stern only weakens his case when he draws a limited parallel between the Kaiser's adventures into world politics and our own "loss of moral confidence and credibility" as a result of Vietnam, or when he urges students not "to confound a moment of repression [in America] with the dark night of totalitarianism [in Nazi Germany]." Such evocations of the anti-war Left's rhetorical style make the reader resistant to a historical explanation that lacks any subtlety.

By Stern's admission, not all Germans between 1870 and 1914 shared these illiberal qualities he catalogues. For obvious ideological motives he excludes the Social Democrats from his condemnation. He might similarly have absolved that segment of the German middle class which clung persistently to the liberal ideals of the nineteenth century (not anachronistically, as Stern might wish, to those of a later age). Their dedication to humanistic education, a religion of ethics, scientific progress, and some form of parliamentary government were all hallmarks of a liberal creed which received as much praise in Germany (even after 1870) as anywhere else on the continent. German liberals have often been criticized for having made their peace with the Bismarckian constitution and with the military monarchy it sustained. It is assumed that they dropped their philosophical scruples owing to the practical economic advantages posed by national unification. And yet, their determination to work within the imperial structure need not be viewed as an act of moral treason. Faced with the absence of a parliamentary tradition like England's, continental liberals often had to console themselves with whatever approximations of parliamentarianism existed in their own lands. Thus German liberals tried to make the best of a semi-feudal constitutional state — much as many French liberals had tried to come to terms with the Bonapartist dictatorship.

Stern maintains that the misfortunes of Germany can be instructive for America, inasmuch as they prove that the absence of the liberal spirit is destructive for a powerful nation. This is a highly questionable assertion. Among the most successful states of the twentieth century have been those that have displayed the least regard for liberty. Have mass extermination and total repression caused the administrations of Russia and China to come apart at the seams? Or if the Germans had decided around 1900 to run their homes and schools in a thoroughly egalitarian way, and (unlike other European nations of their time) to renounce any imperialist ambition, would such conduct have protected them from blundering diplomats in a critical international situation? Much of Germany's history between 1871 and 1914 was dictated by her past acquisitions and by the dynamics of her economic development. In all probability, a weak Germany would have provided France with an irresistible invitation to retrieve the territories she had lost after the Franco-Prussian War. Moreover, the population and industrial growth that took place in imperial Germany threatened an older European order, based on the military predominance of France and the economic supremacy of England. The Wilhelmine Empire would have appeared menacing to her Western neighbors by virtue of her mere existence, although, as Gerhard Ritter has demonstrated, her position was made even worse by her increasing rejection of traditional statecraft in favor of military solutions. Still, the incessant concern of her leaders with national security was partly justified by the disruptive effect of their country's rise to power.

Such considerations may be useful in assessing Stern's observations on the First World War, which plunge him into the most impassioned controversy to have involved German historians for more than twenty years. This controversy centers around the findings of Fritz Fischer, a scholar who, by means of copious documentation, has sought to demonstrate a continuity of political purpose between imperial and Nazi Germany, and to challenge the long-entrenched revisionist views on the origin of the Great War. Disputing the self-serving attempts of the various belligerents to assign sole responsibility for the War to their enemies, the revisionists pointed to the massive failure of international diplomacy as the crucial cause. In America, despite the disagreement of such figures as Bernadotte Schmitt and Hajo Holborn, the revisionists found energetic spokesmen among the students of Sidney Fay and William Langer. And in Europe their efforts culminated in the agreement reached by French and German historians in 1951, which affirmed the joint responsibility of their peoples for the First World War. Basic to most revisionism was the belief that the belligerent governments, including the German, contained moderate as well as fierce annexationist elements, but that due to the increasing devastation of the War, the conciliatory voices once heard in Europe were muted by those that called for a vindictive peace, and both sides eventually gave themselves over to the dream of dismembering their enemy's lands.

Fischer broke with the revisionists, by focusing almost exclusively on those political forces operative within Germany before and during the War. He considered Germany's expansionist policy the most decisive factor in causing the conflict and treated her war aims (to which he devoted his chief work) as inseparable from her aggressive and pervasive nationalism. German society, in Fischer's eyes, was so infected by racist and social Darwinist doctrines that no major political movement, including the socialists, could preserve its ethical integrity. Thus, although the military and civil leadership planned the war by themselves, all parties and classes marched behind them in lockstep. The war aims which gave evidence of the entire nation's will to power, made an appearance as soon as the struggle began, and indeed, the Chancellor, Theobald von Bethmann-Hollweg, although misrepresented as a moral critic of the War, spelled out these imperialist aspirations as early as September 1914. On the basis of these assumptions, Fischer argued that the foreign policy of the Nazi period acquired its peculiar features long before Hitler's rule. It took form during the Wilhelmine era and drew strength from that expansionist impulse which fueled the First World War.

Fischer's views generated considerable controversy in German academic and political circles in the early sixties. Many respectable historians — for example, Gerhard Ritter, Hans Rothfels, and Golo Mann — denounced their inaccuracy and sensationalism. In 1964 critiques of Fischer's thesis began to appear in semiofficial government newspapers — one such piece bearing the provocative title, "Germany Does Not Accept War Guilt Twice." Although such indiscretion is partly understandable, it must be regretted in this instance. For what it did was to turn Fischer (among both the German academic Left and its American rooters) into the beleaguered spokesman for his country's lost conscience.

This, moreover, came at a time when his interpretations were already falling under sharp and effective attack. His treatment of the September program and of Bethmann-Hollweg proved particularly vulnerable, as historians like Ritter and H. D. Erdmann used their research to prove the Chancellor's moral earnestness and the utterly transitory character of his war aims. Meanwhile, scholars like Hans Herzfeld and Egmont Zechlin questioned the attempt to view German war aims as the cause of the War, seeing them instead as the product of a bloody and protracted struggle. In some cases German tactics were designed for the purpose of defeating one enemy with the resources of a second one that had already surrendered, for example, the German plan to fight England from the Belgian and French coasts. Stern concludes that the effect of such criticism has been to cast doubt on Fischer's view of continuing war aims at least in Western Europe. A recent study of German activities in the disintegrating Russian Empire of 1917 and 1918, by the Ukrainian historian Olek Fedyshyn, indicates the absence of any prior war plans in the East, too. Recent investigations of the annexationist designs of the other belligerents during the

First World War also shed unfavorable light on Fischer's method of studying the German case outside a broader context.

In view of this research, it seems strange that Stern maintains (as does Holborn in his introduction to the English edition of Fischer's *Griff nach der Weltmacht*) that "German historians have gradually assimilated Fischer's views." He cites as proof the growing consensus within German scholarship that imperial Germany played a critical role in causing the disasters of 1914. Of course this particular admission came from German scholars long before the Fischer controversy, and it continues to be made by some of his most ardent opponents down to the present. The break of German historiography with self-defensive accounts of the First World War was already underway in the 1950s, as relevant historical documents became available, and as German conservatives as well as radicals felt the need for a critical confrontation with their own national past. The Fischer thesis was not a cause but an expression of this process of reappraisal, but its exponents used the new mood to justify the torturing of documents and even a savage bias against their own country.

While Stern dismisses much of Fischer's documentary evidence, he praises him for having found a "continuity of mood and hope," if not of war aims, between imperial and Hitlerian Germany. Unfortunately, he tries to buttress his defense with mere generalities about German illiberalism and with such assertions as the following: "The idea of war as salvation and as liberation from social and cultural abuses had currency among various writers of other countries as well, but hardly among the leaders of other nations at the time." How useful is the qualifier "hardly" in keeping the remark from appearing utterly absurd? No doubt Stern has never studied the influence of Pan-Slavism at the Russian court. Nor does he seem to have read the imperialistic rhetoric of English parliamentary leaders, or of Sir John Fisher, Lord Admiral of the Royal Navy, who publicly advocated a preventive war to destroy the Teutonic menace as early as 1905.

As another defense Stern suggests that "Perhaps Fischer has strained the continuity thesis, but the counter-thesis which posits all the miscalculations and derailments of German policy in the twentieth century were but accidents is still less satisfying." The argument is sheer sophistry. Plainly, historical knowledge is not to be gained by means of a choice made between two glaring hyperboles, on the basis of which half-truth wears better. Granting such reasoning, an atheist might be impelled to concede the premise that the flesh was fashioned by the Devil rather than by God. After all, it is possible to admit anything, when given a choice between two unreal choices.

The positions Stern takes, however, make sense in the framework of the refugee historical tradition. From this perspective, the study of German history has but two overriding purposes: to be an object lesson to foreigners and to serve as a means of contrition for Germans. For example, those German history surveys assigned to my generation in college — with their interminable references to national failures, lost turning points, and squandered revolutions — resembled prosy religious allegories which describe the sinner's descent into a self-incurred perdition. Such preaching has apparently influenced Stern, who expresses approval of Ludwig Dehio's demand for "unconditional recognition" by the Germans of their "terrible role" in twentieth-century history. Perhaps this role has by now been made to appear too terrible, in the sense that any interpretation of the past that puts the Germans in a particularly bad light can expect an enthusiastic hearing among large segments of the American academic community. This has certainly been true of the responses to the Fischer debate. Here sympathy for a scholar battling against some political opposition to his work came to be viewed as the struggle of an honest and wise radical against the cumulative force of his country's whole evil history embodied in its then-present Christian Democratic regime. The almost ritualized outcries, often sanctimonious and uninformed, that came from American scholars against Germans being unwilling to face up to their past, probably raised more questions about historians on this side of the Atlantic than about those on the other. They showed that it is high time that Americans trained in German history, move beyond the pious hysteria of their teachers, and examine their field outside the realm of bad theology. Insofar as they can manage this, they shall follow in the footsteps of those post-World War II European historians, who in writing on the Great War, decided to bury old axes, and no longer merely to grind them.

2. OSWALD SPENGLER AND THE INSPIRATION OF THE CLASSICAL AGE

Modern Age, Winter 1982

I

In his interwar political tracts and in numerous passages from *The Decline of the West,* Oswald Spengler (1880-1936) identifies himself as a Prussophile and conservative as well as a philosopher of history. Such forms of identity were interrelated throughout his literary career, for both his cyclical view of civilizations and his belief in the spiritual exhaustion of Western culture combined to justify his distaste for modern political values. Contemptuous of the liberal faith in historical progress, Spengler challenged the association of human improvement with individualism and equality. Individual self-determination — that hallmark of artistic and moral modernity — was synonymous for him with social disintegration. In his political statements of the twenties and thirties, he calls upon his countrymen to abandon atomistic capitalism for a corporate economy and for an explicitly Prussian ethic of duty to the state.

As has often been noted, his historical theorizing reveals both depth and inconsistency. *The Decline of the West* presents a mechanistic view of the rise and fall of eight discrete civilizations. Whereas some of these civilizations are only cursorily treated, Spengler bestows particular attention upon three of them: Magian (i.e., Semitic-Hellenistic-Persian), Graeco-Roman, and Western. Of these three, the last two are made the major foci for his two-volume investigation. Spengler asserts that the groupings which he studies underwent parallel developments without interpenetrating. All of them proceeded through an equivalent life cycle, moving from creative and coherent cultures into materially expansive but despiritualized civilizations; none of them, however, supposedly influenced the distinctive character of any other.

20

Civilizations are seen as mutually impenetrable cultures, each creating a unique heritage with its own inherent symbolism.[1]

Thus, classical antiquity, marked by a sense of finitude, brought forth a spatially self-enclosed mathematics (Euclidean geometry), a political constitution designed for city-states, and an art stressing form and balance. By contrast, Western society has always aspired toward the unbounded. While Near Eastern culture exalted depth and interiority, finding its representative in the magus and mystic, and while the classical world glorified Apollo, the god of form, Western spirituality is typified by Goethe's Faust who sought redemption through endless striving. Christianity, in fact, departed from its Magian and classical origins once it had been embraced by those Germanic tribes that invaded the Roman Empire. Expanding monastic communities, the dream of papal empire, and towering Gothic churches all flowed from this Westernized Christianity.[2] Historical consciousness, a mathematics embracing infinitude, and an insatiable thirst for universal knowledge were still other characteristics of the Faustian culture.

Such cataloging of distinctive spiritual traits was made possible, according to Spengler, by his disciplined ability to discern a variety of cultural "physiognomies." Only by an intuitive leap, and not by means of discursive analysis, might the historian comprehend the panorama of world civilizations. Such comprehension became feasible for the first time in the modern West; like Hegel and Marx, Spengler believed that only Western society thinks historically, grasping each experienced moment developmentally in relation to a universal process. Yet, true historical consciousness could only prevail once Western man distanced himself from private conceits. "In the end," Spengler observes, "everyone permits himself to bring to the fore that piece of antiquity that most nearly corresponds to his own interests: Nietzsche pre-Socratic Athens, economists the Hellenistic period, politicians republican Rome, and poets the Empire."[3]

This admonition might suggest that Spengler cautiously rejected any comparison between structurally equivalent but spiritually unique culture-civilizations. But such was indeed not the case. Spengler reveled in civilizational comparisons and repeatedly recommended to his

1   Oswald Spengler, *Der Untergang des Abendlandes* (Munich: C.H. Beck, 1969), particularly pp. 210-277; 282-427 *passim.*

2   *Ibid.*, pp. 234-245; 09-927.

3   *Ibid.*, p. 52.

own generation the moral prescriptions of the ancient and non-Western worlds. His inspirations were vitalist (deriving by his own account from Goethe and Nietzsche); and yet, as Count Keyserling noted, he struggled to reduce universal history to something approaching the "mechanical regularity of a watch."[4]

Each civilization's progress was both fated and predictable; however, not causality but intuition, sacred to the romantics, was made the means for understanding each unfolding life cycle. Spengler has sometimes been depicted as a self-denying metaphysician, scorning what he perceived as a historically conditioned scientific method and exalting intuitive truth, while nonetheless rejecting all specific religious doctrines. He celebrated cultural creativity, yet even while doing so, clung to a starkly naturalist view of humankind. In his political writings, he sometimes compared men to "beasts of prey" and interpreted human activity as programmed responses to instinct and other biological imperatives.[5] These zoological assessments, however, were paradoxically juxtaposed, particularly in *Prussianism and Socialism* (1919), with appeals to social conscience and communal concern.

His most prolific German commentator, Manfred Schröter, would have us look beyond Spengler's incongruous eclecticism to his force as a cultural analyst. According to Schröter, the morphological parallels he drew between diverse civilizations, his sense of both their similarity and distinctiveness, and his arresting picture of Western spiritual decay all suffice to justify Spengler's fame, whatever the defects of his documentation and method.[6] Nonetheless, even the discrepancies in his presentation can be instructive. They underscore dramatically his attempt to be both moralist and prophet within the mechanistic-naturalist framework of his theorizing.

The first volume of *The Decline of the West* was written, among other reasons, to instruct the Germans on what historical paths would be open to them once they had triumphed in the Great War. Volume two, composed in the wake of German defeat, contains heady

---

4   Hermann Keyserling, *Menschen als Sinnbilder* (Darmstadt: Otto Reichl, 1926), p. 164.

5   For a caustic statement of this criticism of Spengler, *ibid.*, pp. 166-174; for a more detached and analytical treatment of this naturalist strain, see Lorenzo Gusso, *Lo Storicismo Tedesco* (Milan: Fratelli Bocca, 1944), pp. 338-347.

6   Manfred Schröter, *Metaphysik des Unterganges* (Munich: Leibig, 1949), pp. 34-50; 221-224.

evocations of Caesarism as the ineluctable solution to urban *anomie*, the rule of money, and, finally, mobocracy. Is it mere destiny in the form of some mechanistically predetermined sociological *dénouement* that we encounter here? Or, is there also, as Schröter and I would both argue, a view of triumphant poetic justice in Spengler's portrayal of a new generation of Caesars who would discipline the mob and chasten the money lenders? In *Prussianism and Socialism*, which he wrote simultaneously with the second volume of *The Decline of the West*, Spengler tries to conjure up his avenging angels by pleading: "We need hardness; we need a brave skepticism; we need a class of socialist ruling natures."[7] As we shall see, he provided profuse instructions on the training of this desired class.

II

What place did Spengler assign to classical antiquity in preparing the West for its future? In the case of Rome the answer appears evident. The introduction to *The Decline of the West* treats the modern West as the antitype to Rome and exhorts the reader to look preeminently to that ancient civilization to know his own historical options and limits. European and American cities are compared to Rome by virtue of their money economies, increasingly deracinated populations, and isolation from rural folkways. "The model for the West can only be Rome. Imperialism is pure civilization. In this phenomenon lies irrevocably the fate of the West. The cultivated man directs his energy inward; the civilized one outward. Thus I see in Cecil Rhodes the first man of a new epoch. He represents the political style of a more distant Western, Germanic, particularly German future."[8] In an even more revealing passage, Spengler confesses: "I believe we are civilized men, not men of the Gothic and Rococo. We must deal with the hard and cold facts of a late life whose parallel lies not in Periclean Athens but in Caesar's Rome. Of great painting and music, Western European man can no longer speak."[9]

---

7   Oswald Spengler, *Politische Schriften* (Munich and Berlin: C.H. Beck, 1934), pp. 104-105.

8   *Der Untergang des Abendlandes*, p. 51.

9   *Ibid.*, p. 56.

Comparing Rome and the West, and, even more, exalting Roman ideals as a model for his own nation and age were both problematic activities for Spengler. If culture-civilizations evolved along parallel, but non-intersecting axes, what mimetic value would Rome have for the West, now condemned to its own form of decadence? Moreover, the Empire's soulless expansion combined with its inner decrepitude did not particularly merit modern emulation.

Spengler himself recognized this, and many of the references to Roman society made in *The Decline of the West* are conspicuously condescending. We are told, for example, that the Greeks possessed a "soul" unlike the Romans who merely used "intellect."[10] *Seele* and *Geist* are the descriptive terms applied to Greek culture; whereas the mere pedestrian *Verstand*, or mere factualness, *Tatsachensinn*, are the highest praise that Spengler confers upon Roman intellectuality. Even more to the point: "One can understand the Greeks without speaking about their economic conditions. The Romans, however, one can only understand by reference to them."[11]

Although Spengler may have had no real affection for Roman civilization, he admitted that it did teach lessons to other *Spätzeiten* that had been dealt equally bad hands. "Rome and Caesar taught more to us moderns of a late period than did Athens, Pericles, and Alexander." There were no longer cultural questions at stake for those societies past their prime. All civilizations resembled each other in their spiritual poverty and material expansiveness. They all contained people who were oblivious to family and honor and who seek power and gain until having to submit to a resurgent state. Since the Romans had done as well with this situation as any people could, Spengler rightly called attention to their practical virtues.

This explanation has undoubtedly some merit, but it disregards his changing interpretation of the Western experience. In his political writings, that experience no longer appears structurally analogous to the classical one. *Prussianism and Socialism* presents the history of the West as a continuing confrontation among three powers with distinctive visions of world empire. Catholic Spain, capitalist England, and authoritarian-socialist Prussia have all developed national missions

---

10 *Ibid.*, pp. 44-48.

11 *Ibid.*, p. 25.

that reflect a need for domination.[12] Supposedly it was instinct that impelled these three peoples toward their future; and yet each one developed an ethic in harmony with its particular destiny. Order and duty became the expressions of Prussia's instinct for obedience, just as individual initiative and free trade were made the rationale for England's economic growth.[13]

Significantly, the struggle which Spengler describes in *The Decline of the West* goes back before the modern era and overshadows his usual demarcation between spiritual culture and material civilization. England is repeatedly characterized as a "pure civilization" and Spain as a now weakened vestige of the once proud religious spirit; and yet "the struggle to the death" among these powers is said to have arisen in the Middle Ages in response to primeval instincts. Prussia and England remain armed with their pre-modern legacies, although, unlike Spain, each one has adapted to civilization. England's Viking rapacity shapes its quest for economic domination, whereas ancestral Prussian sentiments still remain alive in the German respect for authority.

As a political analyst and pleader for the Prussian service ethic, Spengler abandoned the structural rigidities of *The Decline of the West* for a view of Western history as a protracted confrontation. The struggle for Western leadership which he depicts leads, furthermore, to the construction of several historical analogies. One of them is a hypothetical parallel between the West's fate and the Peloponnesian War.[14] Spengler does not dwell at length on this comparison, but a case can be made that in portraying the political division in his own civilization, he takes his format from Thucydides more than from anyone else.

The *History of the Peloponnesian War* begins by discussing the epic nature of the conflict treated. From the outset this war was destined to become "the most noteworthy of events," for it "showed both Athens and Sparta at the height of all their power and seeing the Greek world unite behind each of them, part of it at once and the rest after some deliberation."[15] Thus, the original backdrop is given for Spengler's depic-

12 *Politische Schriften*, p. 90.

13 *Ibid.*, pp. 79-83.

14 *Ibid.*, p. 54.

15 Thucydides, *Historiae*, Oxford Classical Texts A, 1, 1-2. All translations are the author's own. Although Spengler mocked the opening passages of Thucydides' *Historiae* as an "extravagant assertion," they anticipate much of Spengler's own naturalist view of human development. For Thucydides political regimes grew and

tion of the monumental war between Prussia and England, which he believes will ultimately divide Europe, and possibly the world, between two imperial giants. Like the contest which Thucydides delineates, the one Spengler evokes appears to him to have also been fated. It developed out of ancient instincts (for order and plunder) and would only end "with the death of a people or of their culture."

England and Prussia, as described by Spengler, bear some affinity to Athens and Sparta. Like those ancient powers whose rise to eminence Thucydides charts, the two Western countries are differentiated by their *mores* and regimes. Like Athens, an urban center marked by barren soil, England practiced trade and in searching for markets became a naval power. Like Athens, whose population swelled "owing to its incorporation of foreign insurgents," England included among its people sometimes defiant individualists and, like Athens, was polarized between rich and poor.[16] Prussia, like Sparta, combined agriculture with military skills and placed the community above the individual. Spengler also suggests that Prussia was pushed into conflict, as Sparta had been, by the economic expansion-turned-imperialism of its more enterprising rival.

Having been more explicitly made by German apologists during the First World War, this analogy was old hat by the time Spengler alluded to it in 1919. Nor need one assume that he himself had discovered an ancient Hellas as paradigm for Germany's moral renewal. To German nationalists Greece had long represented a humanistic ideal which they hoped to see re-embodied in their own country. In distinguishing German culture, whether from the French Revolutionary legacy or from English bourgeois society, nationalist writers from Johann Fichte

---

declined like natural organisms; and yet he viewed the more recent empires as materially and militarily more formidable than their predecessors. Impressed by the physics of Anaxagoras, he ascribed not only to the natural world, but to history as a unitary process a tendency toward "self-growth (*epidosis eis hauto*)." See G. B. Grundy *Thucydides and the History of his Age*, volume II (Oxford: Blackwell, 1948), pp. 27-29; and Siegfried Lauffer, "Die Lehre des Thucydides von der Zunahme geschichtlicher Grössenverhältnisse," *Spengler-Studien*, ed. A. M. Koktanek (Munich: C. H. Beck, 1965), pp. 177-193. This view of natural increments rendered more believable the "extravagant assertions" about the catastrophic and universal scope of the Peloponnesian War; it also operates as an unspoken assumption underlying Spengler's claims for Western uniqueness. Only the West, according to Spengler, had the material means and the imagination to produce an ecumenical empire; therefore the struggle between England and Prussia was the first intra-civilizational contest of truly universal consequence.

16 *Ibid.*, A, 2, 6-7; A, 6,1-6; *Politische Schriften*, p. 55.

to Moeller van den Bruck, one of Spengler's contemporaries, attributed to their people Platonic and Aristotelian virtues. Like Aristotle in *The Politics*, Fichte during the Napoleonic Wars and Spengler a century later advocated autarchy for their people. By becoming self-sufficient, Germans would allegedly avoid corrupting contact with their materialist neighbors and thereby preserve their indigenous virtues of simplicity and sobriety.[17]

Spengler likewise invoked organic images to describe the essence of Prussian politics; and in so doing associated himself with a tradition of German nationalist rhetoric conceived in the romantic era. His characterization of the Prussian spirit as an "unspoken consciousness that integrates the individual with the whole" had origins, moreover, extending back beyond the romantic past into Greek philosophy.[18] Both Plato and Aristotle identified a sound society with a full integration of all its parts. *The Nicomachean Ethics* views the happiness of the body social as a function of a perfect harmonizing of its constituent elements (*ta mere organike*). And Socrates in *The Republic* considers a well-ordered society analogous to a properly controlled human constitution. "For unlike courage and wisdom which by residing in some particular part renders the [entire] city wise or courageous, this [discipline – *sophrosyne*] can only work once produced by being plainly extended throughout the whole, bringing accord to the weakest, most powerful, and mediocre whether one defines that [accord] as due to will, strength, number, possessions or whatever."[19]

These observations are not meant to suggest that Spengler knowingly drew his political concepts from Plato and Aristotle — or even less that he treated their ideas in historical context. My point is rather that in spite of his professed indifference toward the Greeks and his assumption of their mutually impenetrable cultures, Spengler as a political teacher did apply classical Greek thoughts, however veiled the form in which they came. Among the critics who most vehemently assailed *The Decline of the West* were Hellenophile publicists and professors. Many of them bitterly resented what they perceived

---

17 Two studies which treat this subject are Klemens Klemperer, *Germany's New Conservatism* (Princeton: Princeton University Press, 1957), and Armin Mohler, *Die konservative Revolution in Deutschland 1918-1932* (Basel, 1949), particularly pp. 147-209.

18 *Politische Schriften*, p. 4.

19 Plato, *Res Publica*, Oxford Classical Texts, 432a 1-5.

as Spengler's denigration of classical antiquity, particularly the Greek world.[20] This perception no doubt seemed confirmed by Spengler's greater interest in Roman factualness and imperialism than in Greek thinking.

And yet, what H. C. Butler melodramatically styled "the tyranny of Greece over Germany" may have claimed Spengler as one of its unknowing victims. His longest political tract, *The Reconstruction of the German Reich* (1924), puts forth Greek philosophical teachings in the guise of Prussian-Roman traditions. The first part of his writings castigates a variety of groups whom Spengler blames for his people's moral and political decline: parliamentary parties that plunder the government, bureaucrats avid for pensions rather than public service, and "nonproductive" industrialists who live on government favors while manipulating stocks. Above all, he deplores the absence of strong public personalities, such as Bismarck had been in government, the elder and younger Moltke in the military, and August Bebel as organizer of the German Socialist Party.[21] Being convinced that German political and cultural well-being could only be restored through new leadership, Spengler turns to the problems of educational reform.

He stresses the need for education that aims at discipline (*Zucht*) and not merely at formal learning (*Bildung*). Mocking the German humanistic curriculum with its heavy philological emphasis, he expresses sympathy for the "gifted youth who hungers after the reality of his own years." As for the more traditional educator, "the blessed master in the threadbare frock with his head full of Horace," one such as he "might inspire awe, but only for those still in an age without automobiles or airplanes."[22] The educational plan proposed recommends travel, foreign languages, economics, German composition, history and physics. Philosophy and art are understandably excluded, whereas Greek, an element in the humanistic curriculum, receives no mention at all. The teaching of Latin is given a practical, not humanistic rationale. It enables the young to think analytically, supposedly more so than even "the most rigorous mathematical procedure."[23]

---

20 Cf. *Metaphysik des Unterganges*, pp. 25-40; for a detailed critique of Spengler's generalizations about classical antiquity, see also O. Th. Schultz, *Der Sinn der Antike und Spenglers neue Lehre* (Stuttgart and Gotha: F. A. Perthes, 1926).

21 *Politische Schriften*, pp. 145-154; 214; 216.

22 *Ibid.*, p. 229.

23 *Ibid.*, p. 234.

At first glance there seems nothing in this program to recall Greek educational theories. Indeed an unmistakably vocationalist flavor is perceptible in many of Spengler's suggestions: for example, academic credits be granted for travel and professional internships, languages be taught for their commercial and military use, and students to have an opportunity to acquire degrees on the basis of self-instruction with minimal classroom training.

Juxtaposed with this rudely modern reform, however, are Greek philosophical suppositions. Education is conceived in Platonic terms as *askesis*, for which the German *Zucht* is an exact translation: a training of the self for public and political service. *The Republic*, Book Three, for example, devotes considerable attention to the question of training guardians from earliest youth to oversee an ideal society. Prescribing a proper cultivation of mind and body, starting with music and gymnastics, Socrates recommends an education that culminates in "the recognition of the ideas of discipline, courage, freedom, splendor..."[24] Among his tasks the lawgiver would have to shield his people against "intemperateness [*akolasia*]," particularly in the training of guardians. Like young athletes (*asketai*), and like Spengler's apprentice German leaders, Plato's guardians would come to see that "luxury first breeds intemperateness and then illness, whereas simplicity (*haplotes*) is based on musical discipline in the mind and gymnastic well-being in the body."[25]

Spengler, too, emphasizes athletic fitness in his discussion of educational *Zucht*, and proposes that both industries and places of learning encourage physical recreation. Like Plato and Aristotle, albeit less consistently, he seeks to give education a political-ethical end and to place it in the service of a new aristocracy of talent. Spengler cites as a model for such leadership the traditional Prussian administrator whose severity he describes as the "Roman element in Prussianism."[26] Yet, his stress on leadership formation and his pervasive concern with disciplined political personalities may owe more to Greek philosophy than to Roman administration. Plato, too, had warned against the danger of allowing the morally and intellectually unfit "to meddle" in politics. *The Republic* had anticipated Spengler's charges about the

---

24 *Res Publica*, 402C 1-4.
25 *Ibid.*, 404e 3-5.
26 *Politische Schriften*, p. 219.

German state by condemning the practice of allowing one who is a "businessman by nature" to act as a warrior, legislator, or guardian.[27] Such "alteration and meddlesomeness" were harmful to just government, and Plato considered both plutocracy and democracy as morally and intellectually inferior to rule by the best (aristocracy) or to rule by men of honor (timocracy).

Aristotle also foreshadowed Spengler, the educator, when in *The Politics*, Books Seven and Eight, he discussed the methodical training for political leadership. Like Spengler, he asserts the need for differing educations for rulers and subjects; yet also like Spengler he proposes having future leaders serve others in preparation for the exercise of power. In Aristotle's desired regime (*politeia kat' euxen*), the ruling class is expected to combine practical and theoretical reasoning. Although peace and leisure are preferable to strife and restlessness, Aristotle maintains that only by preparing his people to confront difficulty can the lawgiver ensure their preservation. The military arts are the most suitable activity for the younger members of the ruling *genos* who, enjoying "great physical superiority," are eminently qualified to soldier, just as their elders are to legislate.[28] Regarding warlike societies, Aristotle expresses a judgment similar to Spengler's: "Most of these cities can only survive as long as they fight; once they become possessors, their regime is ruined. They let go of their dye, like iron [swords], while pursuing peace."[29]

Of course, whereas Aristotle intended his comment as a devastating criticism of Sparta ("whose lawgiver [we are told] never taught [his city] to enjoy leisure [*scholazein*]"), Spengler made equivalent remarks partly to justify a bellicose way of life. It is surely not my purpose to blur this difference; nor to deny the higher moral ground from which Plato and Aristotle surveyed political problems as compared to Spengler's

---

27 *Res Publica*, all of Book Four but particularly sections 433 and 434. 433c and d offer a social view largely reproduced in Spengler's idealization of Prussia: a community in which men, women, children, slaves, craftsmen, freemen, rulers and subjects are all bound together by the willingness "to do what each can do best without meddling." German corporatist theory — to which Spengler demonstrably contributed — apparently took its bearings from that organic social model so eloquently constructed in *The Republic*, Book Four: "The city striving for excellence through its own wisdom, discipline, and courage, and the ability of each to accomplish what is in him." (433d 7-10)

28 Aristotle, *Politica*, Oxford Classical Texts, 1332b 14-41.

29 *Ibid.*, 1334a 6-10.

naturalistic and presentist perspectives. Still and all, his political writings do betray the imprint of Greek philosophy in a way that excludes
the possibility of mere thematic overlapping. His practice of turning
to Greece to chart a "Roman mission" for his nation need not surprise
the historian. German thinkers were long ambivalent about two forces
they saw in classical antiquity: Greek theory and Roman rule. German
poets and philosophers of the *Goethezeit* paid tribute to Hellenic creativity and aesthetics; but their descendants living during the Second
Empire deemed Rome, not Greece, a fitting prototype for a political
nation.[30] This German infatuation with Rome might have even affected
the largely apolitical Nietzsche. Despite his praise for Greek tragedy,
his *Twilight of the Idols* exalts Julius Caesar and commends the Roman
will to power which had been expressed through imperial expansion.[31]

Spengler represented a further stage of a politicized cultural consciousness: something which he himself would never have denied
and would indeed have enthusiastically affirmed.[32] Nonetheless, his
use of Greek political and educational concepts shows his endur-
ing link to an older German culture. It was a culture created by such
Hellenophiles as Goethe, Schiller, Hölderlin, the brothers Schlegel,
Herder and Schelling; no wonder that in responding to the first stir-
rings of German nationalism, German patriots still viewed themselves
as a *Kulturnation* based upon analogy to the Greeks. Despite the dis-
covery — which Nietzsche was not the only one to make — that the
Greeks were "the political idiots of antiquity," German educators like
Eduard Zeller, Ulrich von Wilamowitz-Moellendorf, Werner Jaeger,
and Eduard Meyer continued to praise their intellectual and artistic
achievements. At some point in his life, certainly in spite of himself,

---

30 On the slowness of this shift in cultural attitudes, see Richard Benz, *Wandel des Bildes
    der Antike in Deutschland: ein geistesgeschichtlicher Überblick* (Munich: Piper,
    1948).

31 See Friedrich Nietzsche, *Werke*, volume X (Leipzig: Naumann, 1906), pp. 321-324.
    In *Twilight of the Idols* Nietzsche praises "the agonic instinct" and "will to power"
    found among the heroes of Greek epic literature; yet he also condemns Greek phi-
    losophers as "the decadents of Hellenism" while reserving his most effusive eulogies
    for Roman conquerors.

32 On the differences between Spengler and Nietzsche regarding their attitudes toward
    the state, see H. S. Hughes, *Oswald Spengler: A Critical Estimate* (New York: Charles
    Scribner's Sons, 1952), pp. 59-64.

and admirer of political success though he was, Spengler, too, fell under the Greek influence.[33]

---

33 Although there is no direct evidence that Spengler consciously applied classical Greek ideals to his own society, Hans Joachim Schoeps has found a precedent for this practice among the supposed precursors of *The Decline of the West*. Jakob Burckhardt and Ernst Lasaulx, both cultural pessimists and widely respected Hellenists, wrote copiously on the Greek contribution to the study of decadence. Both praised Thucydides and Polybius for their naturalist understanding of the cyclical movement of ancient states; and throughout his historical speculation, Lasaulx in particular reverted to Plato's and Aristotle's pictures of the inescapable derailments of political regimes (*katabaseis kai parekbaseis ton politeion*). For Lasaulx and Spengler, if I understand them, the normative and deviant models for society would both be drawn from among other places, *The Republic* and *The Politics*. See H. J. Schoeps, *Vorläufer Spenglers*, second edition (Leiden: E. J. Brill, 1955), particularly pp. 35-63. On Ernst Lasaulx, see my *Conservative Millenarians* (New York: Fordham, 1979), pp. 110-119; and Stephen Tonsor, "The Historical Morphology of Ernst Lasaulx, "*Journal of the History of Ideas*, 25, No. 3 (July-September 1964), pp. 378-381.

3. THE SACRED ECLIPSED?

The World & I, December 1986

L'éclipse du sacré: discours et réponses
by Alain de Benoist and Thomas Molnar
Table Ronde 1986, 247 pages

This book is a series of discussions between two religious thinkers with shared cultural concerns. Thomas Molnar and Alain de Benoist have both written extensively on the problem of secularization in the modern West.

The attempts by modern states to recognize secularism as a public philosophy and to distance themselves from the symbols of traditional theistic religion represent a striking departure from earlier human history. Almost all past societies, even those few that prohibited the establishment of a national religion, encouraged public displays of religious beliefs. The United States until the 1950s impressed foreign visitors, such as the French traveler Alexis de Tocqueville, as a land that combined religious freedom and pervasive public piety.

Against the tendency toward approved manifestations of piety, a militant secularism has asserted itself in the form of opposition to, for example, nondenominational public school prayer (even silent meditations are disallowed as a form of public school prayer) or public funding of activities associated with religious bodies. The attempt to dissociate religious belief from the polity has behind it influential supporters from members of the Supreme Court and Congress through the media and universities down to teachers' unions. This militant secularism has a clear precedent in the anti-clerical Third Republic in France, which strove to eradicate French Catholicism in the opening years of the twentieth century. The culminating point of raising secularism to the level of public philosophy can be found, of course, in Communist countries where atheism and scientific materialism have become hallowed state teachings.

Molnar and Benoist each stress the unprecedented and problematic aspects of governments and societies suppressing the public expression of religious sentiment. They also speculate about the future of our non-religious society. Molnar argues that because of the constancy of human spiritual needs, even secularism must eventually resemble a religion or yield to a real faith; Benoist, however, believes that the sense of the sacred has already departed from our culture.

It may be useful to note that these two thinkers start from dramatically different premises about religion and culture in the West. Molnar is a traditionalist Catholic who deplores the modernizing tendencies in the church and who even now speaks of Martin Luther with a *frisson d'horreur*.

Benoist, by contrast, is a critic of what he calls "*judeochristianisme*," the monotheistic assumptions and ethical prescriptions that have informed Western thought since the Middle Ages. Identifying himself as a "neo-pagan," Benoist has described Christianity and atheism as two sides of the same coin. The biblical reductionism by which all natural and historical phenomena were traced back to a single divine principle left the world without mystery. The view that there is a single divine author of the world, who stands over it and demands human obedience to his will, caused nature to become desacralized. The cosmic point of gravity in the post-pagan West was no longer the relationship between men and nature or their ancient sacred cities but between the Creator and mankind. As long as men fulfilled the divine commandments imposed on them, they would enjoy divine favor and exercise mastery over nature.

Atheism, as Benoist sees it, represents an exaggeration of certain Judeo-Christian ideas committed at the expense of others. Atheists draw from the Judeo-Christian cosmology its desacralized view of nature, and even their customary veneration of scientific laws is derived from a theology that stresses the objectivity of the universe as the product of a self-revealing Creator. The biblical God and his followers are intended to rule nature without being parts of it, and the achievement of Western atheism is to "dislodge God from his throne to put us in his place and to attempt to construct mimetically a relationship to the world analogous to God's relationship with creation." Atheism is the flattery of imitation that post-Christian man pays to a transcendent deity who orders and regulates a world of his own making.

There is an element of truth in many of Benoist's statements, and the presence of that element makes it hard for Molnar to trap him in what often seems a cat-and-mouse game. For example, Benoist is justified in insisting on the necessary connection between, on the one side, atheism, socialism, and millenialist ideology, all elements of Marxism and, on the other, Judeo-Christian culture. Modernist and postmodernist trends did not emerge out of a cultural vacuum. Nor would they today be so widespread among the educational and political elites unless they had a well-established, historical foundation. Benoist finds that certain contemporary ideologies have roots in the Bible: modern nationalism in the Old Testament, modern egalitarianism/universalism in the New Testament, and political millennialism in both Testaments. Unfortunately, he exaggerates these connections. The Bible does not provide a sufficient explanation for modern ideologies that developed thousands of years after the Bible was written. Since ancient times, devout Christians and Jews have believed in a biblical God without turning into secularists. Benoist is provocative when he describes the early church as "the Bolshevism of antiquity." Yet, though primitive Christians held possessions in common and defended the spiritual dignity of slaves, they did not claim to be either scientific materialists or social revolutionaries. Nor were they as "globalist" as the Roman Empire, which persecuted Christians and Jews and imposed emperor worship on all its subject peoples.

In trying to deal with Benoist's presentation, particularly in the last section, which contains questions and answers from participants, Molnar stresses the value-relativity and pantheism in Benoist's neo-paganism. But Benoist proves an elusive target. He manages to counterattack by accusing the biblical God of alienating men from nature, of generating moral fanaticism, and of driving his followers into ceaseless crusades to change the world in his image. Molnar asks one particularly sharp question about the mechanical nature of ritual piety in the Greco-Roman world. What made a sacrifice suitable (*hieroprepes*), as opposed to unsuitable (*memiasmenon*), was largely unrelated to the attitude or intention of the celebrant. The gods were believed to respond to the ritual itself, independently of the worshipper's virtues or vices. Benoist might have responded by pointing out the similarity between the Greco-Roman attitude toward sacrifices and the one suggested in Leviticus. Although in the Greco-Roman world sacrifices was mainly an external affair, the Hebrews, no less than the Greeks, thought that performing ritual sacrifices without the prescribed procedure was both wicked and dangerous. Benoist might also have pointed to the rules that govern Christian sacraments, particularly in the Roman and Orthodox communions. Here, too, the efficacy of a particular ritual depends upon the manner in which it is done. The violation of the proper procedure affects the validity of sacraments, no matter how well-meaning the participant may be.

Significantly, Benoist makes no such comparison between pagan and Judeo-Christian religions. He is determined to underscore their absolute difference and therefore ignores any points of contact between them. Benoist makes much of the presumed difference between the biblical concept of fearing God (*yeras hashamaim*) and the Hellenic sense of feeling awe (*hazamenos*) before divine mystery. But the Hebrew word for fear, *yerah*, can also signify reverence, while the Greek verb *hazesthai* means to dread one's parents or the gods as well as to stand in awe. Some obvious ethical and theological overlaps exist between the Classical and Hebraic traditions.

I believe that Molnar and Benoist both recognize these overlaps. Their contributions reveal that they are immensely learned in philosophy and the study of comparative religions. In battling with each other, they marshal staggering amounts of erudition drawn from entire lifetimes of reading. Unlike most American intellectuals, they believe that matters of the soul count for more than public policy issues. I tip my hat to both debaters and commend them for discussing the truly permanent things.

All the same, a debating format is not always the best instrument for examining scholarly positions. Sometimes, in the heat of battle, the participants blur or exaggerate what in less bellicose circumstances would be presented with greater care. This is particularly true of Benoist. Still, Molnar tries too hard to play his assigned role, assuming a militant Catholic stance a bit too often instead of displaying his sound knowledge of classical civilization. He depicts primarily an ancient world that was mired in animistic superstition. But surely Molnar knows (I have no doubt that he does) that Greco-Roman religion inculcated reverence for one's city and one's ancestors and, as the French historian Fustel de Coulanges showed more than a century ago, contributed significantly to civic virtue and martial valor. The image that I find in Molnar's presentation of pagan society is at best a fragmentary picture of classical civilization. In other, less polemical circumstances, Molnar would likely be as skeptical of it as I am. Despite these objections, the dialogue between Molnar and Benoist makes for exciting reading. One may hope that sometime in the future university students in religion and philosophy will be encouraged to examine and think about this book. Having to read it may be for them an education in itself.

4. ON "BEING JEWISH"

The Rothbard-Rockwell Report, April 1996

A lead essay by Philip Weiss in *New York Magazine,* "Being Jewish," has evoked considerable excitement in paleoconservative circles, and friends have flooded me with copies of this piece together with requests for my comments. Characteristic of Weiss's main argument is the passage on the magazine cover: "As anti-Semitism fades and Jews assume ever greater prominence throughout the Establishment, it's time for Jewish Americans to let go of the idea that they are outsiders."

Weiss cites the obvious evidence of American Jewish economic and professional success, for example, Jewish overrepresentation in the arts and sciences and among the Fortune 500, and he reasonably concludes that any problem of exclusion which faced Jews in the past no longer exists. What bedevils American Jewry, according to Weiss, are two problems: collective memories of gentile persecution, which have left Jews nurturing an exaggerated fear of American anti-Semitism, and the challenge of an open society, one in which Jews have conspicuously succeeded.

Middle-aged and older American Jews, according to Weiss, are still preoccupied with Christian anti-Semitism while fearing the implications of a tolerant society. "As an American Jew," notes Weiss, "I have a largely unlimited social and professional scope. I'm free to do almost anything I want in this society, including marrying out."

Weiss treats the twin fears of persecution and assimilation as indicative of Jewish alienation. Like Benjamin Ginsberg in *The Fateful Embrace* and Stanley Rothman in *The Roots of American Radicalism,* albeit in less detail, he also speculates on the tie between this alienation and Jewish leftist politics. Weiss cites his own father, a prominent scientist now aged seventy, to illustrate this connection.

The senior Weiss and his wife denounced the judge who sentenced the Rosenbergs as a self-hating WASP Jew. They were also associated with various left-wing causes as an effect of their sense of

38

social exclusion. When the younger Weiss observed to his father that Jews, including (and perhaps especially) liberal ones, vented hatred on Christians, the father typically responded: "We know the harm of anti-Semitism. What harm can there be in a minority's feelings against Christians?" Weiss explains that though his father "is at the top of his field, he still carries memories of unfair exclusion."

Weiss concludes that such resentment no longer makes sense in the economic and professional world he has seen. Here Jews are courted by gentiles and "Young WASPs clamor to work at 'Jewish' investment houses." Moreover, "the political scientist Seymour Martin Lipset notes that charity *doyennes* in New York and Los Angeles recruit rich Jews for most Whartonesque balls." Weiss seems annoyed by the statements about widespread latent Christian anti-Semitism made by the ADL and *New Republic*-owner Martin Peretz. Seeking Jewish unity, such victimologists "invoke a model of Establishment anti-Semitism and Jewish victimization that doesn't exist today." According to Weiss, such types also deny the presence of Jewish clout in the media, journalism, and the entertainment industries. Whenever confronted with an observation about Jewish dominance in these areas, such pleaders denounce the one making it as an anti-Semite or self-hating Jew.

Most remarkable about Weiss's statements has been his willingness to make them in the presence of Jewish organization leaders. He has argued with Abe Foxman about the view of American Jewry as a threatened minority in a hostile country. He has also taken on the Holocaust icon and questioned whether memories of past persecution in a distant land can serve as the spiritual and moral center of gravity for those in patently different circumstances. He has, finally, challenged American Jews' easy acceptance of Zionist rhetoric. Here Weiss has not so much brought up the question of dual loyalty as underlined the irrelevance of Israeli nationalism for Jews who do not intend to move to Israel.

He hints at the problem that Jacob Neusner has raised more emphatically: the striking disparity between pronouncements about Israel and living preferences among self-identified American Jews. Why don't more of these Jews act on the basis of the Zionist positions they at least intermittently profess to believe?

If they think Israel is their homeland and that the U.S. may replicate Nazi atrocities, why do people with such sentiments and anxieties remain around? Equally pertinent for me is the question of how those who subscribe to the Jewish nationalist views of the World Zionist Congress and other Zionist organizations can dismiss as anti-Semitism the charge of dual allegiance. In fact, if one does subscribe to the positions of these groups, one is guilty not of dual allegiance but of a sole allegiance, to another country.

Having praised Weiss for his candor, it also seems necessary to point out the occasional silliness that mars his presentation. He is writing a critique of American Jewish craziness as someone not totally free of its effects. He himself sees anti-Semites creeping out of walls. He identifies Pat Robertson and, by implication, other Christian traditionalists, as anti-Semites and then offers the following description of something he noticed on his honeymoon in Montana five years ago: "A red pickup went by with a country-looking driver, the very embodiment of all the values that my family had kept at bay. Probably not that smart, either. And given the landscape, a Jew-hater too."

Weiss's indulgent WASP wife had just made the saccharine observation that everyone had a right to feel "special," after hubby had harangued her about the "specialness" of the Jewish people, as viewed by his family (and presumably by himself). Clearly Weiss did not believe that a Montana rancher has any right to feel special and, on the basis of a spot check, had summarily condemned him as a "Jew-hater."

His own assumptions about anti-Semitism in the American past and the tough row that his father hoed are equally open to question. Despite what we are led to believe was strong WASP prejudice directed specifically at Jews, the elder Weiss is "at the top of his field." This is not a judgment that could apply to Jews like myself who have tweaked Jewish liberals in today's society, but it is applied to Weiss's father, whose talents carried him quite far among supposedly bigoted *goyim*.

This was the case not only for an alleged victim of prejudice but also for someone described as an enraged left-wing radical seething with hatred for gentiles. How could such a fellow succeed in WASP-dom as imagined by Weiss? Unfortunately what he describes of this now vanished society which I can still corroborate, namely Yale before the late sixties, does not in any way resemble my own memories.

Unlike Weiss's society of unfeeling WASP patricians, the antediluvian Yale I recall, in the early and mid-sixties, had overly courteous Protestants, energetic Catholics, and boorish, resentful Jews. This was especially true of the graduate school where Jews, mostly from New York, yammered constantly about their exclusion (from what?). The *goyim* listened patiently to these complaints, like Weiss's lobotomized "philosemitic" wife, and reassured their Jewish classmates that "things are changing."

All my Jewish colleagues in graduate school, noisy anti-anti-Communists, opposed American capitalist imperialism, but then became enthusiastic warmongers during the Arab-Israeli War in 1967. One Jewish Marxist acquaintance went into a rage that the Israelis did not demand the entire Mid-East at the end of that war. Another, though a feminist, lamented that the Israeli soldiers did not rape more Arab women. It would be no exaggeration to say that my graduate school days resounded with Jewish hysterics at an institution where WASPs seemed to count only as decoration.

Moreover, the record of anti-Jewish discrimination to which Weiss refers, in trying to demonstrate that it is vanishing, was not exclusively discrimination against Jews. It was socially motivated, sporadic discrimination against non-WASP non-patricians. Thomas Sowell shows that its earliest victims were the Scotch-Irish who in the eighteenth century were discouraged from studying or teaching at Yale. Upper-class Yankee dominance there could be seen, according to Sowell, by looking at the South English names of faculty and students into the early nineteenth century — and the comments about predominantly Irish backwoodsmen. And it is often left out of consideration that the quotas on Jewish applicants in the Ivy League was even more restrictively applied against Catholics. The Catholic quotas were often the same as the Jewish ones, though they applied to a much larger portion of the total population.

Having read, with varying degrees of thoroughness depending on the section, Leonard Dinnerstein's history of American anti-Semitism, I find there the same ethnocentric error as the one pervading Weiss's view of the American past. Anything short of equal esteem being enjoyed by all social and ethnic groups is treated as evidence of onerous discrimination. And such discrimination is seen as targeting Jews (or Jews and blacks) specifically, even when directed equally at white Christians. For the thousandth time, it might be useful to repeat a criterion of anti-Semitism first brought to my attention by Murray N. Rothbard.

What is explicitly anti-Semitic must aim at excluding Jews *specifically* from some civic or political or economic right enjoyed by everyone else. Much of what Dinnerstein and Weiss treat as anti-Semitic may result in excluding Jews from some advantage, but not exclusively on the basis of their being Jewish. For example, the colonies of early America would not grant full political or civic equality to those who did not belong to established churches; and later upper-class WASPs tried to keep other groups from attending their schools or working in their firms. Such discrimination was not specifically anti-Jewish, and most of the same exclusion that Eastern European Jews encountered from established Protestants they also had to endure from their German and Sephardic fellow-Jews.

Undoubtedly there was and is anti-Semitic feeling in the U.S., but not enough to justify the constant complaining that comes from Jewish organizations and neocon journalists. Almost all American anti-Semitism, moreover, now comes from blacks, a fact that Weiss tries to sidestep in his comments about the objects of black hostility. Far easier to level the accusation of hating Jews against Montana ranchers who are presumably conservative and go to white churches. Having met such people, I know they are actually far more offensive than Weiss, Foxman, and Peretz could ever imagine. In all likelihood, they don't even think of Jews, and have no interest at all in the authorized obsessions of Weiss's companions.

5. A Post-Liberal America

LewRockwell.com, 17 June 2000

On all sides of contemporary political debate, one key shibboleth is both widely conceded and little examined: that we now decisively have entered a post-liberal phase of American political life. This belief, like all ideological maxims, gets wide assent because of the interests it advances and the ways it serves to strategically narrow debate.

But this glib consensus allows us to sidestep a key definitional question, without which it makes little sense to discuss such legacies at all: What, exactly, do we mean by the American liberal tradition in the first place?

The constellation of ideas associated with this tradition in its original setting – individual rights, limited government, local self-determination – count for little in a polity that promotes rampant dependence on state initiatives and remote federal policymaking.

At its peak of influence, this liberal tradition stood pretty much at odds with everything that now goes by the name of modern liberalism. Where we now look to top-down state interventions to secure our liberties, nineteenth-century liberalism held that we were best preoccupied with cementing local safeguards to protect basic individual rights, such as property, speech, freedom of political assembly and worship. We then sought, in other words, for the state to shield pre-existing goods in our political life; today we look to the state to define those goods for us and to secure them by force of its own prerogatives.

This near-fatal weakening of our liberal heritage was brought home to me dramatically during a Republican primary debate held this February. When a news commentator asked presidential hopeful George W. Bush, a designated critic of big government, how he would encourage more learning in schools, he responded that kids would have to learn during his presidency because the Department of Education would enforce standards.

His conservative opponent Alan Keyes turned toward Bush and explained, in his habitual periodic sentences, that kids should learn out of respect for their parents. Moreover, in any case none of this was the business of federal bureaucrats. Bush, who looked puzzled, did not seem to have any idea of the point that Keyes was making: namely, that in the kind of liberal republic set up by the American founders, responsibility for education resided with parents and not in the national capital.

Even those who run around, as Bush does, complaining about federal overreach can no longer grasp this point. Because of a successful theft, however, the waning of liberalism is not widely perceived as a problem. In fact liberalism has ceased to be identified with the society, or with most of the principles, that prevailed during its heyday. It was the worldview, or at least mindset, of the nineteenth-century bourgeoisie, which survived into the next century in a diminished form, particularly after the coming of universal suffrage and the welfare state.

American liberalism's connection to mass democracy was always a troubled proposition – ranging from the outright hostility expressed by some nineteenth-century liberals, to the desperate hope voiced by other ones that the populace could be made to respect property and the rule of law.

In other words, attempts to understand liberalism by reference to a few rules or phrases overlooks the context from whence it came. This oversight is by now predictable, extending from *The Village Voice* to the Cato Institute and including most political commentators situated in between. On the collectivist left, it has been customary since John Dewey and the Progressive era to distinguish between Old and New Liberalisms, the new being supposedly better because it discards concerns about property and stresses scientific public administration. Individual development is turned here from a family or communal task into one assigned to socializing experts.

On the libertarian side, meanwhile, classical liberalism is now associated with certain exercises of individual will, often involving the use of mind-altering drugs.

The point to be kept in mind here is that bourgeois liberals (in whose world liberalism was defined and practiced) were neither self-actualizing yuppies nor wannabe social engineers. They belonged to a stratified and mannered society, created nuclear families, and typically professed some form of Christian (most often Protestant) doctrine. It is not sufficient for locating liberal ideas to forget about the world that liberals inhabited.

Nor is it reasonable to imagine that one is faithful to such people by pulling out a useful tag from their writings that can be fitted into a transitory policy paper. What they did and said pertained to a class and culture that today exists only vestigially. Moreover, the disintegration of that non-egalitarian world built by liberals owed much to revolutionaries who also called themselves liberals.

Those who like the new model have a right to their preferences, but not one to misrepresent what they are describing. An obvious difference exists between the Parthenon and some house recently constructed with Dorian columns. While the second may have better plumbing, it is by no means an improved version of the first. One can understand neither ancient nor contemporary architecture by viewing Doric structures as imperfect approximations of modern neoclassical homes.

A similar misunderstanding occurs by attaching "liberal" to political schemes that are less and less related to what that term once meant. Having the federal government enforce multiculturalism or help reconstruct gender relations is not a liberal project; it is, rather, a post-liberal one. It is hard to stop this practice because of accumulated mislabeling, going back to liberal social planners in the early twentieth century and to the players of other related word-games, for example those who shifted the meaning of democracy from vigorous self-government, necessarily at the local level, to being administered by professionals, made more sensitive, or indoctrinated in democratic values.

All of this may seem like a semantic exercise or nostalgia (a far graver lapse, in today's ceaseless romance with the idea of progress). But this is only because the issues raised have been successfully muddied. And that is because the twentieth century's most monumental political success, centralized administration, and those who talk it up, hide the true extent of their work.

To get the descendants of once proud Englishmen to surrender most of their earnings to the central state, which now polices insensitive speech and may soon criminalize the same when uttered in the home, is a testimony to social engineering. But it is one made possible by dressing up revolution in reassuring cliché and by holding on to an ornamental monarchy.

Those who submit to this political lobotomization appreciate the appearance of continuity, however little substance remains behind it. Media-approved governmental encroachments on traditional social practices or on property rights are now by definition liberal. Only a fascist – or a noncompetitive presidential candidate – would disagree.

6. THE MANAGERIAL PRESIDENT

Reassessing the Presidency, The Ludwig von Mises Institute, 2001

L egend has it that the U.S. was founded incipiently, if not explicitly as a presidential government. Whether this tendency was already present in the minds of the Founders or whether it emerged as a historical destiny to be ecstatically embraced, an executive regime is what we supposedly were meant to be. An entire school of American historical writing, which has dominated public education since mid-century, elevates presidential power to the skies. Identified with academic celebrities Arthur Schlesinger, Clinton Rossiter, William Leuchtenburg, James M. Burns, and John Morton Blum, this American historiography treats what was best in our past as the work of activist presidents.[1] Individually and collectively, these presidents led our country toward what intellectuals wanted it to be: a social democratic experiment bringing the benefits of our reformed society to a still unredeemed world. This mission is essential to presidential government as conceived by mainstream historians, and all the major conflicts into which our leaders thrust us from the Civil War on, with the possible exception of the Spanish-American War, are seen as morally desirable actions. Though the Vietnam War occasioned doubts for at least some of these historians, who have never been as anti-Communist as they are anti-fascist and Teutonophobic, the storyline has stayed largely the same. International involvement is mandated by morality and our

---

1 Among works that best represent this presidential hagiography are James MacGregor Burns, *Roosevelt: The Lion and the Fox* (New York: Harcourt, Brace & World, 1956); Arthur M. Schlesinger's trilogy, *The Age of Roosevelt* (Boston: Houghton Mifflin, 1956-1960); William E. Leuchtenburg, *Franklin D. Roosevelt and the New Deal* (New York: Harper Torch Books, 1963); *idem, In the Shadow of FDR: from Harry Truman to Ronald Reagan* (Ithaca, N.Y.: Cornell University Press, 1983); *idem, The National Experience* in two parts, contributors John M. Blum, Edmund S. Morgan, Willie Lee Rose, Arthur M. Schlesinger, Kenneth M. Stampp, and C. Vann Woodward, 5th ed. (New York: Harcourt Brace Jovanovich, 1981), particularly the second volume; Richard E. Neustadt, *Presidential Power* (6th printing, New York: New American Library, 1964); and Clinton Rossiter, *The American Presidency* (New York: New American Library, 1956).

global position, and only those who suffer from Richard Hofstadter's
"paranoid style of politics" or Gregory Fossedal's isolationist impulse
reject America's rendezvous with destiny.[2] In Schlesinger's scenario,
the U.S., as fashioned by Wilson, Franklin Roosevelt, and Truman,
defines and upholds a "vital center" positioned between two ominous
extremes: communism and what is a kind of generic "Right." The latter
is a sufficiently sweeping category to take in a medley of evils, from
anti-New Deal Republicans to Francisco Franco and the shattered
remnants of Nazi Europe.[3]

It would be tedious to dwell on this characterization of presidential
America for an obvious reason: we all know it well. Most of us have
had it drummed into our heads by middle- and high-brow cultures
and by American educational institutions. One does not have to visit
Mount Rushmore or look at our coins to get the point: the U.S. is a
land of morally driven, energetic presidents who have made us into
the envy and dread of the world. They have nudged and sometimes
pushed us into assuming international leadership while moving the
furnishings around in our own national home. In the extreme example of this thesis put forth by Harry Jaffa and Gary Wills, our greatest
president — the *sanctus omnium sanctorum* Abraham Lincoln — had
to reconstruct our regime and national purpose to provide us with a
"second birth in freedom." That is the way these historians understand
the Civil War: as a bloody rite of passage into a new America dedicated
to democratic equality.[4]

Such arguments about a presidential America prevailed despite a
very different founding, one that mavericks M. E. Bradford, Murray
Rothbard, George W. Carey, and Forrest McDonald all have focused
on.[5] These and other scholars bring up the embarrassing fact that

2   See Gregory Fossedal, *Exporting the Democratic Revolution* (New York: Basic Books,
    1989).

3   Arthur M. Schlesinger, Jr., *The Vital Center: The Politics of Freedom* (New York: Da
    Capo Press, 1988).

4   Cf., for example, Harry Jaffa, *Crisis of the House Divided* (Chicago: University of
    Chicago Press, 1982) and *Equality and Liberty* (New York: Oxford University Press,
    1965), particularly pp. 82-84; and Gary Wills, *Lincoln at Gettysburg: The Words
    that Remade America* (New York: Touchstone Books, 1993).

5   See, for example, George W. Carey, *The Federalist: Design for a Constitutional
    Republic* (Urbana: University of Illinois Press, 1990), esp. pp. 154-73; Murray
    Rothbard, *Conceived in Liberty*, vol. 4, *The Revolutionary War: 1775-1784* (Auburn,
    Ala.: Mises Institute, 1999); and for me the most compelling indictment of the
    Wilsonian experiment in presidential dictatorship, "War Collectivism in World War

the authors of the Constitution and *The Federalist Papers* assumed they were establishing a legislative republic. This republic would be dominated at the federal level by Congress, not by the president, and certainly not by what Alexander Hamilton called the "weakest of the three branches," the Supreme Court. The preeminence of the legislature seemed inevitable in a republic, and the Founders devoted more attention to that body than to other branches of government, discussing its powers and limits in Article One. The assignment of a presidential veto, in Article Two, was not intended to allow the president to push Congress around but, as indicated in *Federalist* No. 5, was thought necessary "to allow him to defend himself."[6] The need for such a defense, explained Publius, is undeniable in "purely republican regimes" in which "the tendency of the legislature" to overwhelm the other branches is "almost irresistible." In such situations, representatives "appear disposed to assert an imperious control over the other departments; and as they commonly have the people on their side, they always act with such momentum as to make it very difficult for the other members of the government to maintain the balance of the Constitution." Not belief in a necessary and salutary executive supremacy, but a different assumption — namely that presidents would be irreparably weak in republican government — caused the Founders to assign countervailing powers to the executive in dealing with Congress.

A more considered defense of American executive power, made by Straussian authors Martin Diamond and Harvey Mansfield, is that presidential government, though not mandated by the American Revolution or Constitution, came along in the course of time, and that, these authors say, was a happy turn of events.[7] That turn has contrib-

I," in *A New History of Leviathan*, Ronald Radosh and Murray N. Rothbard (New York: G.P. Dutton, 1972). See also Forrest McDonald, *The Presidency of George Washington* (Lawrence: University of Kansas Press, 1974); and M.E. Bradford, *A Worthy Company: Brief Lives of the Framers of the United States Constitution* (Marlborough, N.H.: Plymouth Rock Foundation, 1982); *Original Intentions: On the Making and Ratification of the United States Constitution* (Athens: University of Georgia Press, 1993).

6   Roy P. Fairchild, ed., *The Federalist Papers*, 2nd ed. (Baltimore, Md.: The Johns Hopkins University Press, 1981), pp. 322-23.

7   Cf. Martin Diamond, "Challenge to the Court," *National Review* 19 (June 13, 1967): 642-44; Harry Jaffa, "The Case for a Stronger National Government," in *A Nation of States: Essays on the American Federal System*, Robert A. Goldwin, ed. (Chicago: University of Chicago Press, 1963), pp. 106-25; and Harvey Mansfield, *Taming the Prince: The Ambivalence of Modern Executive Power* (New York: Free Press, 1989).

uted to a more just society and to a more peaceful and democratic world, where American influence has been brought to bear. Such a defense typically cites all the happy outcomes attributable to presidential energy: the emancipation of slaves, the victory of democracy in the two world wars, civil rights enforcement, and New Deal initiatives. Without strong executives at the right moments, they tell us, American democracy and democracy in general would not have survived.

It is fairly predictable what old republican critics of such a view would say in response. In fact, the tracts of Murray N. Rothbard, Llewellyn H. Rockwell, Jr., Justin Raimondo, Albert J. Nock, and H. L. Mencken all serve as illustrations. To wit, that overreaching executive power has made a mockery of the rule of law; that socialism by any other name tramples on republican liberty; and that if the U.S. had stayed out of World War I and had not lied its way into it, the European powers might have been forced to make a peace without conquests. Moreover, continues this rejoinder, Lincoln's war against the South's constitutionally defensible (albeit imprudent) secession cost the American people more than six hundred thousand lives as well as the end of the old republic. Although these respondents would differ in their judgments from the promoters of executive energy, they would all agree on the general picture of what has happened. Both sides look at the rise of presidential power as the major political change since the Progressive Era. Both stress that the consolidation of presidential power took place at the expense of Congress, after a long struggle for federal control between these two branches. One might also perceive an overlap in the way the two sides trace presidential ascendancy, from Hamilton's establishment of a central state with centralized banking and a monarchical president to Lincoln's seizure of dictatorial power to the activist, interventionist executives of this century. Though most would disagree with the triumphalist depiction of this process, they would accept the evolutionary course it highlights, from a congressional republic to a presidential empire. The same process is the object of study in James Burnham's post-war monograph on American congressional government. In the late 1940s Burnham celebrated the legislative branch as "the one major curb on the expanding executive and unleashed bureaucracy. If Congress ceases to be an active, functioning political institution, then political liberty in the United States will soon come to an end." While Burnham ultimately opted for the imperial presidency as a corollary of the American empire that he thought necessary to oppose Soviet expansion, he nonetheless recognized its Caesarist, anti-constitutionalist feature: "Caesar is the symbolic solution — and the only possible solution — for the problem of realizing the general will, that is, for the central problem of democratist ideology." Furthermore, once the "structure of government" in the modern world, including the U.S., moves away from "the rule of law," the only alternative by the "soaring executive" is Caesarism. For the rule of law represented by an effective Congress to be restored, "individual members of Congress [must] have the courage to say no against the tidal pressures from the executive bureaucracy and the opinion-molders so often allied with them."[8]

This author has no problem with Burnham's strictures about presidential power or with his distinction between a republican rule of law vested in Congress and the ensuing presidential Caesarism. It is equally reasonable to treat early American history as belonging predominantly to the first and most of our more recent history as betokening the second. In fact, it may be argued that down to the present century, even vehement assertions of presidential power, for example by John Adams in the Alien and Sedition Acts, by Andrew Jackson during the Nullification Controversy and by Abraham Lincoln, far more cataclysmically, during the Civil War, did not exhaust the republican framework of our government entirely. Movement back in the direction of congressional authority, shared sovereignty with the states, and effective limits on federal overreach usually followed extraordinary assertions of presidential will.

After the Civil War, when a largely Republican Supreme Court struck down Reconstructionist legislation, brakes were put on the central state, by the central state itself. From the Civil War down to the Progressive Era, with the possible and useful exception of the old Democrat Grover Cleveland, presidential power was at least as restrained as it was in the early republic. It is only in the twentieth century that, save for the Harding-Coolidge anomaly, the presidential momentum has seemed unstoppable. Presidential bureaucracy has reached the density of a middle-sized municipality; presidents initiate war basically at will; and a national media and its academic adjunct advocate even further extensions of presidential prerogative, providing

8 James Burnham, *Congress and the American Tradition* (Chicago: Henry Regnery, 1959), p. 344. See also Frank S. Meyer, "The Revolt Against Congress," *National Review* (May 30, 1956): 9-10.

they fit progressive models of social reconstruction. Despite these developments, this writer would suggest a modification of the received conservative view of presidential power. The apparent enhancement of executive authority points to something else. Indeed by now it is principally something else, the expansion of the managerial state.

The American intellectuals and journalists who drool over bumptious executives have no scruples about running down and even unseating presidents when it suits their ends. They will turn around, as Schlesinger and other "liberals" did, and decry the imperial presidency — even when associated with liberal presidents Johnson and Nixon — if they decide they want someone else in the White House. Most of our opponents are no more pro-presidential than the Earl of Warwick was pro-monarchical. They support executives whom they and their friends can jerk around or whom they happen to fancy. It is unfitting to compare such devious opportunists or mere agenda-pushers to divine-right monarchists or to those who, like the German legal scholar Carl Schmitt, believed honestly in executive dictatorship.

Moreover, the executive democracy that our opponents talk up has less and less to do with presidential energy. It does not require willful presidents but demands figureheads who allow the right sorts of strategists to take charge. Those who extolled Clinton's policies would likely have turned on him if he had issued executive orders ending federal antidiscrimination enforcement. What has happened is that most federal administrations are now tied to the executive, so the chattering class prize that branch as the one especially concerned about human rights as opposed to mere republican liberty. This contention is not gainsaid by the fact that President Clinton saved his political neck and enhanced his popularity by exaggerating the size and ferocity of the Religious Right. The relevant question is whether President Clinton would have remained a powerful political force if he had decided to act in a way that offended the media and other parts of the political class. Would he still have enjoyed his level of support inside and outside of the government if, say, he had embarked on the restoration of a constitutionally limited republic, i.e., one that took the Tenth Amendment seriously?

Such rhetorical questions must be asked if we are talking about a plebiscitary Caesar of the kind described by James Burnham. Such a leader must have real scope for his actions and is the same as someone who merely presides over a managerial empire. This is not to deny that presidents in the past contributed to the unmaking of constitutional government, but such is no longer the case because of frantically energetic executives. Our presidents are becoming Scandinavian monarchs, photogenic front men for a managerial dictatorship. While Danish and Swedish kings in the past crushed local liberties and instilled servile habits, their descendants function as decorative art for socialist governments. They make public appearances and dutifully read speeches that are prepared for them by unfailingly leftist administrations. In a way, that prefigures the current American presidency: place-holding monarchs reign while administrators rule.

But our executive may be more problematic. After almost a century of constitutional derailment bringing cumulative power to the office of president, both the possibility and the temptation to abuse that office exist. If the abuser cultivates journalists and the permanent administrative state, he should be able to get away with considerable mischief. Each time the president steps forth to call for collective atonement for racism, sexism, and homophobia, he encounters diminishing public objection and resonant media approval. Today most Americans do not care if the same president who inflicts quotas and sexual harassment suits on other white males takes gross liberties with female employees. What for others is a public disgrace and a costly crime is for him a private matter. For tens of millions of Americans (mostly black and female), it is outrageous that one dares even to judge the current political correct occupant of the Oval Office. Whatever else may have caused this suspension of ethical judgment, it is related to our cult of the president. The German president, who is a largely powerless windbag given to preaching on the burden of German history, does not have the resources to become a Clinton-like deity. He is a proper figurehead intended to be little more. We would do well to imitate this practice and not to allow our executives their present cultic status.

The most that can be said in favor of energetic presidents is that they resemble willful monarchs of centuries past. Because of their unfettered energies and contempt for constitutional restraints, they have increased not only their own influence but the imperial sway of their country. This does not justify adulation for the presidency in general or for its recent depraved place-holder any more than, say, admiration for William of Orange should predispose one to empower Prince Charles to invade other countries or to punish the sexism of his subjects. An argument can be made that presidents should be forced to accept the original limits on their power. To this the response from Charles Krauthammer and *The Weekly Standard* would be that an emasculated presidency leaves the U.S. vulnerable.[9] This of course begs the question, "vulnerable to what?" Are we speaking of an invasion from Latin America or the incursion of Middle-Eastern terrorists? Both are now happening with presidential support and partly because of the immigration policies endorsed by the conservative opposition. Besides, lamenting a weakened executive branch is a bit like worrying about the future barrenness of teenage recipients of welfare if we discourage underclass fertility. Let us worry about present excesses and not conjure up hypothetical alternative ones! All the same, any attempt to control the presidential mystique will surely fail unless sufficient actions are taken to rein in the federal bureaucracy. Administrative tyranny will continue to rage no matter under what branch of the federal government. It can thrive as easily behind a congressional shield as a presidential one, and it can behave arbitrarily in either case.

One of the most cloying tributes to presidential arrogance ever devised is the deprecation of Dwight Eisenhower in the revised edition of Clinton Rossiter's *The American Presidency*. According to Rossiter, Eisenhower "came to the office with practically no thoughts about its powers and purposes. ... He had swallowed a good deal of the propaganda directed at Roosevelt and Truman, and the result was a first year in office during which his view of his powers was not much different from that announced long ago by William Howard Taft."

Rossiter scolds Eisenhower "for asking congressional approval in 1955 for the authority to defend Formosa and the Pescadores." Because of his quaint belief that the president was "under a stern moral obligation" to ask congressional support for the deployment of troops abroad, Eisenhower was willing to "cripple the striking power of the presidency in a sudden crisis." Rossiter believes that "history will likely judge Mr. Eisenhower's leadership to have been the most disappointing of all" because of his failure to expand executive power in two areas: "his abdication of both moral and political leadership in the crisis of integration in the South and his refusal to push steadily for solutions of the crisis of education throughout the union."[10]

---

9   See, for example, William Kristol, "On the Future of Conservatism," *Commentary* 103 (February, 1997): 32-33; and Charles Krauthammer's "The Lonely Superpower," *The New Republic*, July 29, 1991, pp. 23-27.

10 Clinton Rossiter, *The American Presidency*, p. 124.

Rossiter despises Eisenhower for not going far enough both to impose federal control over learning and to reconfigure the social life of the American South. But what he blames on Eisenhower's "modest conception of the presidency" — the failure to engage in grandiose social engineering — no longer hinges on the person of the chief executive. Rossiter's plans for the American presidency can now go forward at an accelerated rate, because it has been turned over to bureaucrats, judges, and opinion-wrenchers. The presidency has at last been turned into a bureaucracy under Caesar's banner, with a debauched chief of state cast into a mock imperial role.[11]

---

11 For a study of the managerial ascendancy in American government and its effects on the presidency, see my *After Liberalism: Mass Democracy in the Managerial State* (Princeton, N.J.: Princeton University Press, 1999), esp. pp. 49-71.

7. THE GOOD OLD ORDER

Modern Age, September 2002

England: An Elegy
by Roger Scruton
Pimlico 2001, 270 pages

England: *An Elegy* is one of a number of similar books to appear around the turn of the millennium which lament the unraveling of a particular European nation or of Western civilization more generally. Works such as John Laughland's *The Tainted Source*, Peter Hitchens's *The Abolition of Britain*, Yves-Marie Laulan's *La Nation Suicidaire*, Eric Werner's *L'Après-Démocratie*, and a host of works published by a conservative German press, Hohenrain Verlag in Tübingen, trace this unraveling to such contemporary forces as social engineering, consumerist frenzy, multi-cultural politicians, or popular indifference to an inherited way of life.

Roger Scruton's study stands out from the others of its kind owing to two features. First, Scruton is interested in celebrating the English past — which was still at least vestigially present in his youth — more than in diagnosing the crisis at hand. The last section of his book, "The Forbidding of England," does dwell on the war waged by the powers that be against the English past, especially its moral-religious traditions and the hereditary parts of the English constitution, but the focus of his work lies elsewhere. He is primarily engaged in depicting the scenery, traditional worship, literature, and national character of a people that have ceased to be what they once were. He is trying to explain to thoughtless contemporaries just what was *good* about the old order they have destroyed.

Second, Scruton brings to his subject not angry sarcasm but a moving, elegiac tone. While another much-publicized lamenter, Peter Hitchens, praised Scruton's threnody in the newspaper *Express on Sunday*, there is nonetheless an enormous difference between the retrospective views of Hitchens and Scruton. In *The Abolition of Britain*, Hitchens finds everywhere dreary scenes, class privileges, and tasteless food in English life in 1973, the point at which he begins his narrative; in effect, he stipulates from the start that the "good old days" were not so good. Scruton, however, has unbounded affection for the land of his childhood. He hopes to show that the "warts" of the now-lost past actually contained hidden virtues, deserving of lament.

Both writers were born to working-class families, but Scruton, unlike Hitchens, thinks happily about the private school he attended on scholarship and about the education and fellowship associated with an English upper class now in disarray. He dwells on his connection to High Wycombe Royal Grammar School — its "carcass of Gothic arches," its devoted teachers, its emphasis on English manners — and the continuation of his then already established way of life when he went on to Cambridge University. While Scruton does not romanticize mid-twentieth-century England or its still largely unspoiled country-side, he recalls a more desirable society than the one that Hitchens does not seem really to miss, save for the multicultural nightmare that is now taking its place.

It seems to me that Scruton presents the more plausible view of an older English society, certainly the one that I remember from living in England in the late 1960s. Scruton is undertaking a task that would be more difficult for his French, German, or (dare I say) American counterparts, none of whom can be as firmly anchored in continuing traditions persisting into the second half of the twentieth century. German conservatives now inhabit a once heavily bombed and then physically rebuilt country. The Germans were subject to "re-education" after a totalitarian leap into darkness, first by democratic conquerors, and later by Germany's own triumphal Left committed to "overcoming" the national past. In France, one discerns a similarly disjunctive situation. Given France's pock-marked history — that is, a succession of republics, years of Vichy collaboration that serve the same function for the French Left of creating national guilt, as Hitler does for German "*Gutmenschen*" — and an oozing Communist-Stalinist subculture, it is hard to find an authentic living past that the French Right can convincingly show is being threatened.

In the United States, an equally unpromising set of conditions plagues the historically-minded Right. Here the official conservatives celebrate democratic-capitalist innovation, while offering minimal resistance when the center and the Left advocate the stripping away of "insensitive" historical symbols, particularly those of the American South. When its most prominent patriots define the United States as the enemy of other peoples' traditions and as the icebreaker of global democratic revolution, it is hard to make Americans believe in the inspirational model of the past. The "conservative mind" that Russell Kirk tried to trace for his country is the last thing such an uprooted society would care about. A heavily consumerist "universal nation" has little interest in holding on to its Euro-American antiquities, especially when its multicultural elites treat the Western past as a source of shame.

Scruton's elegy makes clear how strongly the English incorporated and depended on their past, even their distant past, until recently. And he is not just speaking about scattered traces of peasant life that social democratic bureaucracies have not yet plowed under. Nor is he identifying the English past with the "heritage" industry or the "historic districts" that are periodically refurbished to allow for political sensitivity. Instead, he is recalling a social-religious-cultural totality that took form in the Middle Ages and survived vigorously into the world of his youth. Perhaps this continuity and the accompanying anachronisms, Scruton says, have aroused the irritation of some Anglophobes, but that totality evinced virtues that now appear permanently barred to us.

An American reader might take away from Scruton's work two general impressions. The first concerns the necessarily close relation between England and Great Britain. Despite England's history of warring with her Celtic fringes, her association with Scotland, Ireland, and Wales has also formed her people. From shared genes to the rich contributions made by her non-Anglo-Saxon subjects to her evolving national heritage, England is hard to imagine without her predominantly non-English lands. Moreover, the English monarchy is a British one, into whose symbolism and titles have been woven Welsh, Irish, and Scottish themes. Indeed, the English monarchy as a defining national institution is based on the concept and reality of a Great Britain already diminished by the twentieth-century loss of Ireland. Scruton speculates on the high price that might have to be paid for the continued "integration" into Great Britain of the overwhelmingly leftist Scottish and Welsh electorates. Such discontented voters will likely go on supporting the Labour Party, which is pushing the policy of devolution while radicalizing England and obliterating its national identity. Scruton underlines what can only be described as a Catch-22 situation.

The other impression that I extracted from Scruton's recollections is how *little* the England of fifty years ago resembled the America of my youth. Despite fashionable talk about an "Anglosphere," the English society Scruton portrays is recognizably medieval in its religion, countryside, architecture, and class structure. It is not a country founded by Protestant sectarians who neither had nor desired a medieval past and whose descendants have turned into celebrants of Progress, commerce, and human rights.

American Anglophiles such as T. S. Eliot, Henry James, Allen Tate, and Russell Kirk were aware of these differences but occasionally sought to blur them by referring to the overlaps between the English-speaking peoples. While these undoubtedly existed, they have also been overstated, usually for political reasons. The British themselves hurried to uncover such links when they tried to harness America's transatlantic power to offset the ascending might of their German cousins. As we know, such a task yielded dividends. Americans, and especially American Protestant patricians, in both the North and the South, wanted to think of themselves, as John Lukacs observes in *The Passing of the Modern Age,* as belonging to a British world. Though much of this WASP establishment sprang from German, Dutch, and Huguenot settlers and lived in a country with heavy German, Irish, Hispanic, Italian, and Slavic concentrations, English society and English culture in the twentieth century provided for well-born or well-bred Americans the models of choice. And, among other things, this determined America's taking of sides when Europeans went to war in 1914.

But this balance of influence would change eventually. In the last thirty years, the period covered in Hitchens's book, the English would reinvent themselves, it may be surmised, partly because of the overshadowing presence of their American allies. Today English, like continental European, progressive thinking reflects what is going on across the Atlantic, with a time lag of a few years. Ray Honeyford's *The Commission for Racial Equality* (1973) shows how closely England's attempt to build a "multiethnic society" patterned itself on American reforms and American visions. Europeans and Canadians both welcomed visible Third World minorities and then applied to them the principle and practice of compensatory justice that Americans had adopted in dealing with the descendants of former black slaves.

Like the Austrians, who in the nineteenth century went from controlling the Prussians politically and, to some extent, socially into becoming a weak sister, the British have fallen into a steadily diminishing status in relation to the United States. In the past American patricians strained to ride to the rescue of England; today the English can be expected to rally instantaneously to American foreign policies, while couching their endorsement *comme il faut* in the rhetoric of the one Anglophone superpower. Such a relation tells us less about the durability of a "democratic" friendship than about who pays whom the flattery of imitation.

Particularly the English Right has indulged in the fantasy that by making their country a junior partner of the United States they will be saved from a teutonized Europe. This strategy, based on fear, which Margaret Thatcher has expressed repeatedly, betrays the outdated perspective of the Second World War. By now Germany is a guilt-obsessed, politically correct giant that is trapped in the bureaucratic labyrinth known as the European Union. The Germans, who tell the world incessantly that national identity is obsolete, should serve as an example to Englishmen, as John Laughland wisely observes, of what his countrymen should *not* do, unless they wish to abandon their national destiny entirely. In the meantime, in the real England, for better or worse, the United States is the dominant foreign power. Militarily, culturally, and economically, the world Scruton describes has made way for an American colony, run by a prime minister who sounds eerily similar to recent American presidents.

There are two opinions expressed by Scruton that merit critical attention. While English governments in the past behaved toward the Irish unjustly and in some cases brutally, it is unwise to speak of a "justified enmity" that the Irish feel toward the English. The Irish have benefited as well as suffered from their ties to England, as certainly have the English from being associated with those across the Irish Sea. The industrialized English Midlands abounds in transplanted Irishmen and their descendants, who are now, like the native Englishmen, coming into conflict with the more recently arrived Pakistanis. For generations Anglo-Irishmen and emigrating Irishmen have done profitable things in England besides working in factories and mines. They have made careers in English politics, commerce, journalism, and literature, going back to the age of Edmund Burke. Surely enmity should not characterize the relations of these intertwined nations.

It also seems that Scruton may go too far in justifying the socialist politics of his father Jack Scruton, whose radicalism is attributed to "romantic feelings" and misguided patriotism. While filial piety has much to recommend it, it is foolish to gloss over the connection between the Labourites in the 1940s and 1950s and the social changes that Scruton deplores. A persistent loathing for traditional English institutions, identified with "privilege," caused Jack Scruton and other English workers to become the foot soldiers of the post-war socialist reconstruction of their country.

Without the votes and enthusiasms of all those who felt socially deprived, the Labour Party could not have made war on the English educational system, the hereditary parts of the British constitution, including the monarchy, and even the national architecture. If for no other reason Labour and its followers should be despised for covering England with a disfiguring rash of workers' dwellings and other concrete memorials to state planning. One need hardly mention the loss of historic liberties brought about by English socialism. While Scruton may therefore write tenderly about his kin (as a conservative should), others may be justified in holding more critical opinions about his vehemently Labourite family.

Despite these isolated reservations, one must conclude that Scruton has produced in *England: An Elegy* a small masterpiece. A respected formal philosopher who has written erudite works on Kant's aesthetics and on the history of philosophy, Scruton has now exhibited a further talent, as a graceful memoirist and as the chronicler of what we are told is an England which is now gone.

8. GERMANY'S WAR WOUNDS

The American Conservative, May 2003

The expressions of opposition to the war with Iraq from German Chancellor Gerhard Schröder and from his foreign minister Joschka Fischer have evoked on the American side outraged responses, from complaints that Germans do not appreciate all we did for them to neoconservative attributions of Nazi motives to the current German pacifism. Against this background it might be useful to note the appearance of three books in the last four years, by novelists W. G. Sebald, Günter Grass, and by military historian Jörg Friedrich.

Grass devotes part of his newest book, *Crab Walk*, to the Soviet torpedoing of the *Wilhelm Gustloff*, a ship full of German refugees in the Baltic that went down with 8,000 passengers on January 31, 1945; in a less novelistic fashion, both Sebald and Friedrich take on the bombing of German cities from 1941 until the end of the war. Of the two books that treat the bombing, Friedrich's *Der Brand* (*The Fire*) is the more densely documented, and though written like spasmodic news dispatches, the more factually relevant study of something that should not have happened. Sebald's *On the Natural History of Destruction* combines a moral indictment of German novelists and historians for sidestepping the mass murder of their people with reminiscences about growing up in the post-war German rubble.

All three books, which are being sold together on German Amazon, have received favorable treatment in the German national press and, remarkably enough, in the leftist *Der Spiegel*. The association of Grass, a Noble Prize recipient, with the pro-Communist Left for forty years probably has not hurt and may have neutralized objections from German intellectuals that he is making the Germans appear to be "victims." Some of the same built-up grace may be working for the other two authors, who have published on the Jewish victims of Nazi persecution. Although Friedrich's book, unlike the others, has not been translated, conservative German papers have given it loads of attention. And so did his most acrimonious foreign critics in the British *Daily Telegraph* who laced into Friedrich for suggesting that Churchill, the most admired of all English statesmen, was a war criminal.

What Friedrich demonstrates, from the recorded statements of Sir Winston Churchill and the air commanders Sir Charles Portal and Sir Arthur Harris, is that British leaders from 1940 on intended to bring Germany to its knees by wiping out civilian populations. Whereas 567 Englishmen died in the much-publicized bombing of Coventry (and about 21,000 in all of the German bombing of England), the Anglo-American side, and particularly the British, destroyed in the range of 650,000 German civilians. Most of this went on in the final year of the war, when German cities were relatively defenseless and the British side had abandoned the argument that it was destroying weapons and war matériel in favor of the idea that it was waging a "moral struggle." In the final section of his book, Friedrich details the destruction in wartime Germany of artwork, collections of priceless books, monuments, and churches. Among the most spiteful of such destructive acts was the firebombing, on April 17, 1945, of the complex of buildings that had until 1918 formed the Prussian royal residence and the surrounding town of Potsdam. In all, 1,700 tons of bombs were dropped over a few square miles, until they had obliterated 47 percent of the historical buildings and killed 5,000 residents. Although this malicious act had no conceivable effect on the already decided outcome of the war, it allowed the British command to express disdain for "Prussian militarism."

The massive use of phosphorous bombs, when they became available as a weapon of choice, was turned with deadly effect against the historic sections of German cities and villages. Although these *Altstädte* had little if any military value, their stone and wood structures were easily destroyed, thereby causing the indiscriminate devastation that the firebombing was supposed to create. Churchill and Harris hoped to develop this aerial warfare effectively enough to bring death to at least 100,000 residents of a German city. Despite repeated efforts, particularly in the Northwest corner of the country, between the Maas and the Ruhr, the British bombers failed to get their kill. But among the totals they did achieve were 45,450 killed in Hamburg in July 1943, about 25,000 in Berlin, after several years of intermittent bombing, and 35,000 fully identified dead and about the same number of *Teilidentifizierte* (partially identified corpses) killed in Dresden on February 13, 1945. What kept these figures from getting even larger, according to Friedrich, were the high degree of German civilian morale and the continued operation of *Flak*, the German Aerial Defense Unit. British attempts to win the struggle by smashing German morale did not work; although by 1943 most civilians had grown contemptuous of the German Ministry of Propaganda, they also believed they were fighting an implacable enemy. Thus Berliners did what they could to stave off aerial attacks, and when there was little they could do to keep the bombers away, hid in well-insulated bunkers.

In *The Atlantic Monthly*, Christopher Hitchens, who shares at least two neoconservative fixations, residual Teutonophobia and a passion to bring democracy by force, looks at those German authors who have begun to dwell on German suffering during World War II. A friend of Sebald's, Hitchens is upset that his fellow writer would be so carried away by his subject. Those Germans who told Sebald about their wartime agonies show "a combination of arrogance and self-pity tinged with anti-Semitism."

Sebald supposedly indulged in similar self-pity when he spoke about the "war of annihilation" against German cities. Hitchens is deeply shocked at the way he mourns the *Luftwaffe's* crew slightly more than he regrets the raid on Norwich. Unfortunately for his outlook on the war, Sebald was living in a North German town that had been targeted for obliteration. And the losses the inhabitants endured in his part of Germany vastly exceeded, on a scale of ten to one, those that the British sustained during the Battle of Britain.

The commentators on British firebombing, however, did not contribute much toward the opposition to the Iraq war being expressed by the Red-Green coalition in power. Friedrich and Sebald have produced books that would be more characteristic of the fifties and sixties than of the present age. Hitchens is dead wrong when he remarks "the peaceful and democratic reunification of Germany has impelled or permitted Sebald and other writers to revisit the half-hidden past." Forty years ago, West German politicians and historians were not shy about uncovering Allied atrocities against Germans. Back then neither the anti-fascist thought police, now shielding their countrymen against national pride, nor compulsory German self-hate held back historical research.

Most importantly, the German Left and the East German Communist regime had a vested interest in playing up the Western Allies' bombing of German civilian populations. The Americans and British maintained both armies and weapons systems in West Germany in order to contain the Soviets and their East German allies. The most bloated figures for the number killed by the British in the attack on Dresden — 300,000 — came from the assistant chairman of the East German Council of Ministers in 1955. In 1977, the *Soviet Encyclopedia* cooked up the more modest (but exaggerated) figure of 120,000. By contrast, West German authors wrote tracts without reservations not only on Anglo-American bombing but also on the murder, mayhem, and rape of the Red Army as it moved through Eastern Germany.

Neither Schröder nor Fischer nor the leftist press that endorses them wants any part of the present attempt to bring up atrocities perpetrated on their countrymen by the Allies. They treat these killings as necessary to free Germany from fascism, a process they are continuing by providing tax money to agencies and organizations that expose and harass German nationalists and those who do not accept Germany's place in the new world order. Fischer, who once aided the Bader-Meinhof Gang and then grumbled at German reunification, is the Teutonic Jane Fonda, an ostentatiously self-hating German who has published ten booklets to express his revulsion for his own country and his hope that it will soon disappear. During the Serbian crisis, Fischer, like his mentor, the cultural Marxist Teutonophobe Jürgen Habermas, looked forward to the "replacement of classical international law based on nations by a new cosmic regime built on human rights." To present such a figure as a German chauvinist is either an act of lunacy or colossal ignorance.

Unlike the struggle against Serbia, in Iraq the United States declared war against a Third World government, which means, for the multicultural imagination of the German Left, against an object of veneration. Fischer would think differently if the enemy were Jörg Haider's Austria. It was he who led the way in calling for international sanctions when the anti-immigrationist Haider was entering an Austrian coalition government four years ago. At a time when over 80 percent of the German population opposed American military action against Iraq, and as high a percentage opposed the American use of German bases, it would have been imprudent for any German politician, including Fischer, to be associated with the Bush administration. But that is not the same as suggesting that critics of the American war policy are thinking about what happened in the 1940s. Most of them were not around at that time; in any case contemporary Germans live in a society in which all pre-1945 German states are treated in the same negative way that our media depict the Confederacy. Finally, it has to be mentioned that given the presence of about seven million Muslims (out of a total population of 82 million) in Germany, over 60 percent of whom vote for the Left, the Red-Green coalition is pursuing its interest by protesting the waging of a war against a predominantly Muslim country.

The themes of Friedrich's and Sebald's books resonate most among two groups: older Germans who lived through the events they describe and the anti-globalist national Right. Both may have been targeted by what Hitchens styles "the right-wing mass-circulation tabloid *Das Bild*," which "has called Churchill a war criminal and is serializing Friedrich's work." When the German nationalist weekly *Junge Freiheit* asked readers who lived through the firebombing to contribute accounts of their experiences, the editors were flooded with narratives. Meanwhile, other German newspapers have begun the same practice, with the same results. Living through the *Brand* is a demonstration of the "will to endure [*Durchhaltewille*]" that elderly Germans talk about the way Nazi and Soviet victims discuss their near-death experiences. Curiously these elders welcome comparisons with those who survived the Holocaust and distinguish their wartime trials from the Nazi government that helped to bring about the invasion of Germany.

But there is also the anti-war Right, which extends from the Christian Democratic dissidents Peter Gauweiller and Willy Wimmer and their followers to the anti-immigrationist *Republikaner*. Representatives of this persuasion oppose American imperialism and fall easily into invectives about Tony Blair as an American lapdog. On this embattled Right, resistance to the war goes hand-in-hand with memories about Allied bombing. Nor is there any affection on the nationalist Right for the Red-Green opposition to the Bush policy, which is seen as having nothing to do with specifically German interests. American globalists are right to hate and fear such types. Unlike Fischer, they are not waiting for the German nation to go away and, unlike the Christian Democratic majority, deeply resent any view of their people as moral pariahs.

9. WAR AND DEMOCRACY

The American Conservative, August 2003

Power Kills: Democracy as a Method of Nonviolence
by R. J. Rummel
Transaction Publishers 2002, 246 pages

R. J. Rummel's most recent book abundantly documents the costs of arbitrary rule. The author cites statistical evidence that underlines the suffering caused by tyrannies down through the ages. We are warned against political masters seeking to control our lives and to confiscate our possessions. The message conveyed is that power can be lethal; and though the figure of 170 million political murders for the twentieth century (given in an earlier book, *Death by Government*) may be questioned, Rummel is teaching, or so it appears, a valuable lesson about democidal regimes. He believes such bad governments do not come along where "democracy" has been firmly established. In "well-established" or "undoubted democracy," we are told, leaders feel accountable to protect the lives and liberties of their citizens. Also since "about 1800" democracies, with a few "insignificant exceptions," have not gone to war against each other. The more thoroughly democratic these governments have been, the less likely they are to start shooting at one another.

Rummel concludes that "democracy" leads toward "democratic nonviolence" and so it is therefore desirable that "democratic" governments triumph everywhere. His fixation on a single model of government makes one think of the Marxist-Leninist concept of "peace." In both cases, tranquility can only prevail after the rest of the world has modeled itself on the revolutionary pacesetter. Without the imposition of this prototype, we are made to believe, violence must go on and on. Although "democracies," like people's republics, are not supposed to make war on one another, they do fight necessarily against those who conspire against the Good. The fault is not theirs, of course, but that of their opponents, who arouse justified anxiety about "keeping the world safe for democracy."

Rummel, whose *idée fixe* has afflicted Michael Ledeen, Walter Berns, William Kristol, and Michael Mandelbaum, and rages at the American Enterprise Institute and the *Wall Street Journal*, supplies a definition of democracy that is far from rigorous. Everything we should value — free markets, pluralism, periodic elections, easy access to citizenship — are essential for the received concept of "democracy." Such a conceptual hodgepodge indicates a lack of familiarity with one of Aristotle's key distinctions in *Metaphysics* (Book Five) between what is essential and what is accidental in a particular being. There is nothing intrinsic to popular government that requires a free market or that protects private property against political confiscation. Pre- and non-democratic governments existed almost universally until the twentieth century, and both arrangements in the Western world protected private property and supported capital formation. Rummel also leaves out of his celebratory picture what is ideologically inconvenient: that Western democracies have now developed gargantuan public sectors, are turning into supranational bureaucracies, tax their subjects up to half or more of their earnings, undertake massive social engineering, throw dissenters into jail or ruin them professionally for making politically incorrect remarks, and, in short, behave less and less like constitutional regimes.

The designation "democracy," once ascribed, confers irreversible grace on the bearer. Thus England and the U.S. have always been democratic, even when they did not conform to Rummel's criteria. When they protected slavery and aristocratic privilege, they were nonetheless pilgrims on the way to the earthly Heaven. Others, like the Germans and Austrians, are made to appear inherently totalitarian. Rummel finds nothing good to say about his ancestral people, even though the German and Hapsburg Empires before the First World War provided for universal manhood suffrage, affirmed the equality of all imperial subjects before the law, and in the German case had a highly federalized system of government. As two of their critics note in *Orbis*, democratic globalists operate with an "upward and downward ratcheting tool." Countries that please them get high grades for democracy no matter what. But those they hold grudges against can never reach the bar of acceptability unless American social engineers have managed to reconstruct them.

An even moderately well-read historian should have a field day pinpointing the questionable assertions in Rummel's book. For example, does it make sense to tell us that the Confederate States were not a democracy because Jefferson Davis "was appointed by representatives of the states" as president? This was also the process by which the American Electoral College once functioned, and indeed indirect election of the executive continues to be the practice in Israel, Germany, Italy, and among other members of Rummel's democracy club.

Furthermore, Rummel argues, "from 1914 to 1915 Italy, the liberal member of the Triple Alliance with Germany and Austria, chose not to fulfill its obligations under that treaty to support its allies. Instead, Italy joined an alliance with Britain and France, which prevented it from having to fight other liberal states and then declared war on Germany and Austria." Italy, which was arguably no more "liberal" in 1914 than were the other members of the Triple Alliance, was not obligated by its purely defensive alliance to become a belligerent. Technically, Germany and Austria had struck the first blow. Its nationalist foreign minister Giorgio Sonnino, moreover, did make an offer, which also contained a threat, to support Italy's former allies. The hitch was that Austria had to cede territories in the Tyrol and along the Adriatic that Italian expansionists viewed as "unredeemed Italy." When the Austrians understandably refused, Sonnino negotiated with the British government the Secret Treaty of London. This pact stipulated those Austrian and Turkish territories that Italy would be free to gobble up if its government declared war on Germany and Austria. Rummel's interpretation of these events exemplifies his idiosyncrasies. The post-war attempt to pay off "liberal Italy" with territory inhabited by non-Italians inflicted undemocratic hardship on millions of Europeans.

Pervading Rummel's historical overview is a conceptual error that Paul Craig Roberts stated about someone else reviewed in this magazine: "Freemarket democracy is an intellectual construct that nowhere exists." What Rummel does is throw together characteristics he would like to see in his ideal society and projects them onto the chosen few. Anglophone countries, regimes that have been allied to the U.S. and England (minus Stalin's Russia), and societies he considers sufficiently pluralistic all make the grade. Many of his judgments about who is or was democratic are almost childishly anachronistic, for example pre-capitalist aristocratic societies and slave-owning ancient cities with highly restrictive access to property, and he generally ignores the tendencies of modern mass democracies to strike at capitalist and pre-democratic constitutional arrangements. Does it make sense, for example, to refer to the present German, French, or Swedish governments as supporting a free market, given the high degree of public control of the economy, the size of the public sector, and the amounts of direct and indirect taxation? (On this development Rummel should consult the works on European taxation and European administration by French economist Yves-Marie Laulan.) And how "democratic" are the current highly centralized Western regimes in which bureaucrats in Brussels can take away the historic liberties of an Englishman in Manchester? While no one is denying that life in a Western country is better than growing up in Chad or Yemen, the abstract superlatives Rummel attaches to his own society and to its past and present allies are overblown.

Nor does he convince me that countries that fail to pass his "democracy" test are necessarily dangerous and in urgent need of reconstruction. Some countries have modernized themselves in a more belligerent fashion than others, and some do export terrorism and exercise "power that kills." But other societies, like Thailand, Singapore, Jordan, and Morocco, have authoritarian governments that do not pick on their neighbors, nor are these regimes conspicuously brutal to their subjects. Meanwhile the U.S. — as a "democratic" empire builder — bullies and cajoles Eastern Europeans into electing "democrats," who often, as in the cases of Hungary and Croatia, were connected to the Communist secret police but are nonetheless held up as reliable instruments of American globalism. Such guided democracy, John Laughland observes, is seen as indispensable for keeping Europeans insulated against "nationalists." Rummel creates the impression that those who resist this forced re-education will sooner or later commit mass murder. In the more complex world that exists, however, that is not the case.

While Rummel has much to say against political cruelty, his own prescriptions for avoiding it are as questionable as his view of the Euro-American past. Seen through his Manichaean filter, humanity is divided between good and bad countries with good and bad histories. It is incumbent on the righteous to overthrow and rebuild societies they consider reprobate. Contrary to his stated purpose, Rummel may be goading the dogs of war, and, according to those precursors of modern political theory Thomas Hobbes and David Hume, such creatures are especially troublesome in the hands of popular governments. A retired professor from the University of Hawaii, Rummel fits in with the bacchanalian democrats who celebrate his work at the *Wall Street Journal*. Like them, he seems a sedentary throwback to the Jacobins of the French Revolution, who were equally intent on crushing pre-democratic authority. Thus the Jacobins eagerly slaughtered 30,000 "counter-revolutionaries" on the guillotine and over 100,000 Catholic peasants in Brittany and the Vendée. These mass executions, whose number Rummel not surprisingly understates, included small children.

Like him, the Jacobins were hurrying to advance universal democratic "peace." However, what the Surgeon General says about cigarettes applies here as well: democratic globalists "can be hazardous to your health."

10. For Zionists, Time to Choose

VDARE, 12 November 2003

In a provocative essay in *The New York Review of Books* (October 23), "Israel: The Alternative," New York University historian Tony Judt depicted the idea of an exclusively Jewish state as an "anachronism," "rooted in another time and place." He wrote:

> "At the dawn of the twentieth century, in the twilight of the continental empires, Europe's subject peoples dreamed of forming 'nation-states,' territorial homelands where Poles, Czechs, Serbs, Armenians, and others might live free, masters of their own fate. When the Habsburg and Romanov empires collapsed after World War I, their leaders seized the opportunity. A flurry of new states emerged; and the first thing they did was set about privileging their national, 'ethnic' majority — defined by language, or religion, or antiquity, or all three — at the expense of inconvenient local minorities..."

He went on:

> "But one nationalist movement, Zionism, was frustrated in its ambitions. The dream of an appropriately sited Jewish national home in the middle of the defunct Turkish Empire had to wait upon the retreat of imperial Britain: a process that took three more decades. ... The problem with Israel, in short, is not — as is sometimes suggested — that it is a European 'enclave' in the Arab world; but rather that it arrived too late. It has imported a characteristically late-nineteenth-century separatist project into a world that has moved on..."

Judt, however, added that Israel is different in one key respect from its European prototypes. It is a democracy, "hence its present dilemma" in having to dominate the Palestinians against their wishes.

Judt argued that this situation has created serious difficulty for Jews outside of Israel. How can Jews who extol "pluralism" — by which Judt seems to mean "diversity" — in their native lands simultaneously defend an Israeli polity that rejects that "pluralism"? And what happens if Americans start believing that "Israel's behavior has been a disaster for American foreign policy?"

Judt's gloomy conclusion: "The depressing truth is that Israel today is bad for the Jews."

Judt saw two major strategic alternatives for the Israelis:

1. *Maintaining an ethnically-specific nation-state.* In this case, they have to choose between three tactical options: a) trying to dominate the currently controlled area, with its ominous demographic problem. Or, b) retreating to the pre-1967 boundaries — in effect trading demographic for geographic risk. Or, c) keeping the current area and expelling the Arab populations. (He made it clear he thinks this last quite possible.)

But Judt preferred his second major strategic alternative:

2. *Abandoning the nation-state ideal*: "The time has come to think the unthinkable ... a single, integrated, binational state of Jews and Arabs, Israelis and Palestinians."

He argued:

> "Israel ... is an oddity among modern nations ... because it is a state in which one community — Jews — is set above others, in an age when that sort of state has no place .... In a world where nations and peoples increasingly intermingle and intermarry at will ... where more and more of us have multiple elective identities and would feel falsely constrained if we had to answer to just one of them .... In today's 'clash of cultures' between open, pluralist democracies and belligerently intolerant, faith-driven ethno-states, Israel actually risks falling into the wrong camp."

Having committed this incorrectness, Judt is now in the crosshairs of a powerful lobby. Andrea Levin of *The Jerusalem Post* wrote that Judt (who is Jewish) was "pandering to genocide." On *National Review Online*, David Frum accused Judt of "genocidal liberalism," noting "one must hate Israel very much indeed to prefer such an outcome [a binational state] to the reality of liberal democracy that exists in Israel today."

And the assault on Judt goes on: only on Monday, *National Review Online*, continuing the magazine's new role of Likudnik lickspittle, published an extraordinary demand from *The Jerusalem Post's* Saul Singer that American "[e]ditors and producers should be as intolerant of such musings as they are of racism, and for the same reason: Both reek of the genocides of the last century." Note that this censorship only applies to the U.S. In Israel, such notions are debated all the time.

But should Israel be regarded as a "liberal democracy" without accepting demographic developments which many Zionists apparently deem appropriate to Western countries? Alan Dershowitz, in his recent mini-book *The Case For Israel*, never allows that there is a case to be made for ethno-national Christian states as well as for a Jewish one. Abe Foxman, Edgar Bronfman, Tom Lantos, and their legion of counterparts in Western Europe apparently propose quite separate paths of development for the Jewish and Christian states. They apparently think that Israel is entitled to an interwar style path of ethnic particularism. The West, however, is ordered to take a de-ethnicized path.

One very recent example of this double standard has just occurred in Italy. The president of the Union of Italian Jewish Communities, Amos Luzzatto, scion of a distinguished Italian Jewish family and a relative of Mussolini's first minister of finance, insisted (in an interview on October 23) that Jews, like all European peoples, need to have "their own established seat [*insediamento ebraico*]." But Luzzatto, who has remained close to the Italian Communist Party, previously gave quite a different interview to the *Corriere Della Sera* in June 2002. There he passionately attacked the opponents of Third World immigration to Italy, linking them, without proof, to the fascist past.

It is not surprising that Judt is catching hell for bringing up this double standard.

I believe there were errors in Judt's stimulating brief. Contrary to his reflexive disdain, most of the interwar successor states of the fallen European empires practiced some fair measure of liberal government, although they did tend to treat ethnic minorities as second-class citizens — just as Israel has always done.

Moreover, Judt's binational state concept, familiar as the Communist prescription for Arab-Israeli relations thirty years ago, is only an option if the Palestinians as a whole are willing to drop their terrorist activity. This may well not be the case.

Most interestingly, despite his appeal to current trends in the West, Judt actually wants something quite different for Israel. In a "binational" state, there are two continuing nationalities. But Judt approves of modern Europe because it consists of "pluralist states which have long since become multiethnic and multicultural. 'Christian Europe,' *pace* M. Valéry Giscard d'Estaing, is a dead letter; Western civilization today is a patchwork of colors and religions and languages...."

He dismisses, with breathtaking arrogance, those Europeans who object to this process:

> "A minority of voters in France, or Belgium, or even Denmark and Norway, support political parties whose hostility to 'immigration' is sometimes their only platform. But compared with thirty years ago, Europe is a multicolored patchwork of equal citizens, and that, without question, is the shape of its future."

Note carefully, however, that the only "patchwork" that Judt envisaged for Israel is a checkerboard.

Nevertheless, even this is definitely not good enough for David Frum. He makes it clear that, beyond his (very reasonable) concerns about the security aspect of Judt's proposal, lies his ambition that Israel remain an ethnic state. Yet this is the Frum who notoriously raged against Sam Francis in "Unpatriotic Conservatives" (*National Review Online*, March 19, 2003) for advocating "a politics devoted to the protection of the interests of what he [Francis] called the 'Euro-American cultural core' of the American nation."

Jewish and white Christian liberals are not interchangeable. They become liberals in response to different social and psychological needs. Jews are inclined to be multiculturalists because they fear and distrust a Christian majority. White Christians, if one follows the argument of my book *Multiculturalism and the Politics of Guilt*, chase after "diversity" because they are self-dismissively throwing away their civilization. If it is true, as Judt asserts, that Christian Europe is now a "dead letter," this is because its population became as guilt-ridden and as self-loathing as European-American Christians.

A final point needs clarification. Judt equates "democracy" with multi-ethnicity and multiculturalism. As a political theorist for many years, I remain astonished by this already ritualistic association. Why does being "democratic" require opening one's borders and welcoming in a cultural "patchwork?"

Certainly this requirement would have struck Aristotle, Rousseau, Montesquieu, and Thomas Jefferson as disconcerting. These political thinkers assumed a high degree of homogeneity as essential for popular self-government.

I believe that American Zionists should be reconsidering their inconsistent positions, instead of ganging up on Judt. Abe Foxman and the Anti-Defamation League, for example, make themselves ridiculous and vulnerable when they denounce those who oppose the granting of drivers licenses in California to illegal immigrants as far-right anti-Semites — while they simultaneously defend Israel as a "Jewish state."

Tony Judt's politics are not mine. I believe that Israel should remain predominantly Jewish and that the U.S. and Europe should remain predominantly Euro-American — and I support whatever is necessary to achieve these objectives. But, unlike his hysterical opponents, Judt believes that what is sauce for the Christian West must also be (more or less) sauce for Israel. He is at least an honest Jewish liberal.

11. WRONG REVOLUTION

The American Conservative, February 2004

America the Virtuous: The Crisis of Democracy and the Quest for Empire
by Claes G. Ryn
Transaction Publishers 2003, 221 pages

A work by a prolific Swedish philosopher now living in the U.S., *America the Virtuous* is a hard-hitting assault on the "neo-Jacobins," who devote their energy to plotting war against "states that pose little or no military threat to the United States or the rest of the Western world." Ryn zeroes in on the ideological motives that actuate such militarists. In the process he examines the thriving illusion that democratic virtue can be spread universally by forcing American fashions on other peoples. Because of this belief among journalists and politicians, traced at least as far back as the presidency of Woodrow Wilson, the American constitutional republic, and its moral capital, has suffered damage. While Ryn does not claim that a "quest for empire" is the only thing wrong with our culture, it typifies the inability to practice self-government, which requires self-reliant citizens fortified by moderation. In the early twentieth century, Harvard humanist scholar Irving Babbitt (1865-1933) stressed the destructive effects of self-indulgent politics, whether humanitarianism, an insatiable lust for power, or a combination of both, represented by democratic imperialists. Rather than seeing a contradiction between sentimentality and the drive toward world control, Ryn, like Babbitt whom he quotes repeatedly, treats the two as compatible.

America the Virtuous has received proper attention in a syndicated column by Paul Craig Roberts. This former undersecretary of the treasury describes Ryn as a "learned, insightful, and courageous scholar who ably explains the ideas that are destroying our country." Ryn has gone after "ideas that are the property of neo-Jacobins" who call themselves neoconservatives, "a clever euphemism behind which hide groups of radicals who stand outside of, and opposed to, the American tradition. The U.S. has been subverted from within, as these counterfeit conservatives hold the reins of power in the Bush administration." Ryn shows the neoconservatives to be anything but lovers of the past, except in the special sense of hoping to continue their creative destruction, and in a previous book *The New Jacobins* and in a lead article published in *Orbis* (Summer 2003) he makes no secret of his revulsion for "counterfeit conservatives." His critical distinction between modest, constitutionally articulated self-government and the centralized, imperialist democracy unleashed by the French Revolution is carried over to old-fashioned American conservatives and their neoconservative adversaries. And the author comes up with chilling quotations from neoconservative "policymakers" Charles Krauthammer, Ben Wattenberg, and Michael Ledeen, which illustrate their bombast and phony machismo. His sarcastic dissection of a "virtuous" democratic America that is losing its capacity for self-government is certainly worth reading — at least several times. Even in those areas in which genuine progress has been registered — medicine and technology — the result, according to Ryn, has been state managerial control. Without the state being put in charge of everyone's life, we are made to believe, people will not obtain health care or will go on eating junk food and smoking noxious weeds. Without the state controlling income and production, citizens, we also hear, will not be able to enjoy technological advances. Ryn bids us worry about the restoration of real virtue and our political well-being instead of inflicting our nation-building on others.

An unsettling revelation in this study, which is also found in Andrew Bacevich's critique of American globalism, is how far back our present obsessions run. As Ryn demonstrates by bringing up Woodrow Wilson and other Progressives, something closely resembling neoconservatism was already detectable in the early twentieth century. And even more controversially, Ryn quotes the utopian rhetoric about America in Thomas Jefferson, a practice by which he has offended some Southern conservatives. But Ryn's intention is not to throw together the Virginia patrician with those who have praised American wars as experiments in democratic education. Rather, he wishes to prove that radical revolutionary ideas can be found in an otherwise respectable American founder, who had once indiscreetly

talked up the French Revolution. Ryn is demonstrating the long-estab-
lished receptiveness in our society to what now passes for "American
values."

America the Virtuous never answers directly why the politics it
censures have come to characterize self-described American conservatives. Why does the media Right even more than the media Left
embrace radically anti-conservative thinking, particularly on foreign
affairs? Ryn deals with this worrisome question in his closing chapter
by indirection, by stressing the overlap between "abstract universalism" and "a nationalism that is prone to self-absorption and therefore
disdain for others and bellicosity." "Unbounded nationalism" and "a
monopolistic ideological universalism that scorns historically formed
societies" are in fact two sides of the same coin. Both deny the right
of other peoples to be left alone and insist that unless "America the
virtuous" is forcing its will upon other countries, in an endless quest
for empire, there can be neither peace nor justice.

In the '70s and '80s, the American Left swarmed with despisers of
the U.S., which was then engaged in a global struggle against the Soviets
and their proxies. The Right by default became America-boosters, in
whose ranks coexisted both traditional anti-Communists and neo-Jacobins. But it was the neo-Jacobins who by the end of the Cold War were
able to define the moral substance of the struggle against the Soviets,
as a global democratic crusade tied to a particular state representing
a political creed. Unlike other nation states, neo-Jacobin America is
ethnically and racially pluralistic but imagined to rest on a universally
applicable proposition, that everyone should be viewed as equal and
be empowered to enjoy human rights. Ryn recognizes the danger of
what Burke characterized as an "armed doctrine," an invitation to wipe
out historical heritages that displease those legislating for "humanity."
Thus the American Right has come to instantiate two interrelated evils
that belong properly on the Left, anti-historical universalism and revolutionary nationalism.

To his credit, Ryn does not flee from the modern world into a "tra-
ditionalism of a romantically nostalgic, unimaginative or rigid kind"
and speaks of the need to adapt "those elements of traditional Western
civilization that are enduringly valid" to the present age. Nor does he
reject the need for universal ethics, as opposed to the dogmas of the
terribles simplificateurs, those who cannot tolerate having questions
raised about the values they seek to stuff down others' throats.

Lest one doubt Ryn's complaints, recall President Bush's speech to the National Endowment for Democracy, the neocon Congregation for the Propagation of the Faith, that calls for greater financial and human investments in the Middle East until all its oppressed women have been granted full political participation. Peter Brookes of the Heritage Foundation has been endorsing this speech in a widely distributed op-ed piece "Forward Freedom." According to Brookes, we are beset by a "misguided mindset" that believes that democracy is not a "universal value." In fact, Brookes insists, "It is the right of all people — Muslim or not" to live in a "secular, tolerant, and democratic" society. For better or worse, however, such a society was not mandated by our founding fathers, who allowed the several states to maintain their established churches and, with only few exceptions, never advocated political equality for women. Moreover, the French Jacobins, who were candid sexists, would have recoiled from Brookes's gender egalitarianism. In contrast to the active social role played by aristocratic and bourgeois women before the French Revolution, the Jacobins limited female participation in public life to comforting soldiers and bearing sons, who would eventually become *soldats revolutionnaires*. What the new Jacobins described by Ryn are pushing is the universal acceptance of what we now consider as "democratic," an extended yuppie society featuring liberated women, consumer choices, and something approaching open borders.

It is not "a misguided mindset" but the recognition that some social preferences are relative to time and place, and may not be particularly good to start with, that causes Ryn to resist this neo-Jacobin utopianism. Brookes also extols "two of the world's most successful free societies," post-war Japan and Germany, which American social engineers were allowed to resocialize. Aside from the fact that Brookes's fellow-neocon Ralph Peters has just finished complaining that the Germans are almost uniformly pro-Nazi, and aside from the problem that German jails are full of politically insensitive authors, Brookes overlooks the historically obvious: unlike Middle Eastern countries, Germany and Japan had considerable middle classes by the early twentieth century. Both countries, but especially Germany, could point to functioning parliamentary institutions before their stumbling into mischief in the 1930s. (Southern and Southwestern Germany had more liberal constitutions in the early nineteenth century than did any other part of Europe then.) Even more relevant, the U.S. only got to reconstruct these countries after bombing their civilian and military populations back to the Stone Age. Does our Heritage Foundation "foreign policy" maven call for a similar strategy to set things right in Iraq and Saudi Arabia? Ryn laments the presence of a poor "historical sense" among the neo-Jacobins. Indeed in a sequel to this work, *A Common Human Ground*, he criticizes their unwillingness to learn from historical experience, which they claim "provides no moral direction." This observation may be overly generous. Ryn's subjects should not be allowed to talk about "history" until they can learn about what happened in the past.

Incidentally, the real Jacobins produced polished rhetoric, in contrast to those indigestible phrases churned out by their modern counterparts. Ryn does not further our aesthetic pleasure by routinely beginning each chapter with clunky quotations from his subjects. If only we did not have to read them in the original!

12. BOURGEOIS RADICAL

The American Conservative, December 2004

Adorno: A Political Biography
by Lorenz Jäger
Yale University Press 2004, 235 pages

Lorenz Jäger's biography of Theodor Adorno (1903-1969) is a useful study of an unpleasant but influential figure. From the 1920s until his death, Adorno was the prime mover behind the aggregation of cultural and social iconoclasts known as the Frankfurt School. Together with his more down-to-earth co-organizer Max Horkheimer, who contributed family wealth to their enterprise, Adorno took his socially radical think tank, the Institute for Social Research, in 1934 from its interwar home in Frankfurt to New York and later Los Angeles. In 1949, at the urging of Horkheimer, who was then rector at the University of Frankfurt, he returned to his native city to resume their research activities uncovering the bourgeois sources of "fascist" and "pseudo-democratic" pathologies. During their American wartime stay, the two friends also collaborated in the compilation of a bulky anthology of disquisitions dealing with the allegedly fascist mentality of the American population. This work, *The Authoritarian Personality* (1950), had far-ranging consequences for American educators and social reformers despite its turgid and preachy prose and the dubious proofs extracted by the authors through primitive interview techniques.

The Adorno depicted by Jäger was a man of many parts — a philosopher, a sociologist, a talented pianist, and an enlightening commentator on twelve-tone music. His social radicalism took shape after the First World War but not for the reasons that his interpreters sometimes mechanically provide. Despite having a Jewish father — whose name, Wiesengrund, he exchanged for his mother's maiden name, Adorno — it is hard to find evidence of the writer's exposure to anti-Jewish discrimination before suffering dismissal as a university instructor by the Nazis. Adorno was raised in a wealthy home as a Catholic and during his youth was deeply drawn to the religion of his French mother. Despite a professional setback under the Nazis, he was not personally harmed and freely left and then returned to Germany before deciding to immigrate to the United States. This fact should be duly noted in view of the unceasing references in Adorno's work, and in that of his colleagues and disciples, to an omnipresent Nazi danger, which they imagined to be well established in the United States.

After the war, Adorno praised the Soviet Union and the governments that it set up in Eastern Europe as an "anti-fascist necessity." Nonetheless, he made no effort to move to an "anti-fascist" place of refuge, and when he left his adopted country, which he scolded for its anti-Communist hysteria, he did so with documented reluctance. Moreover, notwithstanding his supposed loathing for bourgeois privilege, Adorno lived sumptuously to whatever extent his circumstances permitted. His "untimely death" (as his passing is described in Yale Book News) occurred while he was away from his wainscoted offices on a periodic visit to a resort near the Matterhorn. And for all his talk about the oppression of women in late capitalism, and despite his frumpy appearance (as revealed by the photo on the covers of both the German and English editions of this book), this feminist champion cheated persistently on his wife of many years, Gretel, who, if truth be known, looked less plain than he did.

Jäger's biography is the fairest and most accessible study known to me of this complex, obnoxious thinker. His German prose, which in the original text contrasts favorably to Adorno's, is a pleasure to read, and the English rendering is solid. As in his cultural commentaries, which appear in the *Frankfurter Allgemeine Zeitung*, Jäger here shows considerable knowledge of music, an interest he shares with Adorno and one that might have drawn him to his subject. And though he goes through Adorno's major works of social criticism and correspondence with his soulmates, much of Jäger's work is on the aesthetic side of Adorno's life, which is the least familiar to the radical scholar's American votaries.

As the dust jacket to the German edition explains, Adorno lives on as the social commentator who created the term and criticized the phenomenon of the "culture industry." He was among the first to have grasped as a social-historical critic the destructive power of consumerism in trivializing genuine literary and artistic accomplishments. Jäger shows with abundant quotations how Adorno came to view culture in his own time in much the same way that literary modernist Ezra Pound had, as an industrial commodity or consumer product. He also lets us know Adorno's shocked reaction to the destruction wrought by Allied bombing upon returning to live in his native city of Frankfurt. Jäger quotes his subject's dismay when he discovers that the church in which he had been confirmed, St. Catherine's, has been devastated, together with other local places of worship.

What for me is most remarkable about this biography is the measured way in which its author approaches his subject. Someone whose conservative Catholic convictions and revulsion for political correctness are evident in his other writings, Jäger could not possibly share Adorno's demonstrable contempt for bourgeois Christian society. Indeed, it is hard to read this work without noticing the prevalence of such contempt in Adorno's correspondence with other members of the Frankfurt School. The correspondents express their hostilities, which in some cases seem to stem from an ostentatious sense of Jewish marginality, in a variety of desperate radical positions, from hating their own country long before the Nazis rose to power to pouring affection on Communist dictatorships.

Jäger also relates Adorno's involvement in a project undertaken for the U.S. High Commission soon after his return to Frankfurt, a series of group surveys intended to ascertain the "fascist sympathies" of Germans then undergoing American-led re-education. Adorno's chosen assistants, some of whom themselves had shady pasts in the Third Reich, blurred the distinction between Nazi sympathies and certain well-founded observations about the recent past. Germans who complained about the Allied bombing of civilian populations during the war or about vindictive American treatment afterwards, or who noted the harsh provisions of the Treaty of Versailles ending the First World War, were presumed to be sympathetic to Hitler or else mentally troubled German nationalists. But these damning observations were defensible, as Jäger makes clear, and were fully shared by former anti-Nazis, for example German Social Democratic leader Kurt Schumacher, who had spent the war years in a Nazi concentration camp. In his search for enemies on the Right, Adorno had become the shrillest voice of the American victors at the same time as he was defending Stalinist aggression in Eastern Europe.

But Jäger also documents that Adorno expressed the same attitudes and emotions that he condemned in his fellow Germans. He too was disturbed by the amount of rubble that the Allied bombing left behind. Moreover, he exhibited profoundly bourgeois taste in literature and art, an unfashionable aversion to Negro jazz, and a nineteenth-century sensibility that kept creeping into his aesthetic judgments. Jäger depicts in his subject a cultivated man of learning who was at war with himself and whose internal conflict had a fateful impact on the lives of others. In the late 1960s, in a crisis that might have caused his physical deterioration and led to his death, Adorno was targeted by the student Left at the University of Frankfurt, who broke into and disrupted his classes. Like other revolutionaries before and since, this aging academic was accused of harboring reactionary impulses and of not sincerely opposing sexism. In an orgy of confused symbolism, female protesters bared their breasts in Adorno's sight while waving pages torn from his tract *Negative Dialectics*. Adorno had apparently not done enough to explore the dialectical possibility of shocking German burghers. Significantly, Jäger shifts away from this student unrest to a view of the Matterhorn as seen from the French Swiss region of Valais, a view that he, Goethe, and Adorno all enjoyed. By electing to end on this note, he is making a statement about what Adorno should be remembered for, namely, his appreciation of natural and artistic beauty.

But this really won't wash. What has been called "cultural Marxism" (inaccurately, given its lack of Marxist substance), and which flourishes in Europe and to a lesser extent here as political correctness, would be unthinkable without Adorno and the Frankfurt School. Thanks largely, albeit not exclusively, to their activities, bourgeois normality, belief in God and patriotism have come to be linked in academic culture and among social reformers to a slippery slope leading to fascism. Marxism, which had previously been primarily concerned with economic revolution, was transformed through Frankfurt School guidance into an unrelenting war against patriarchy, Christianity, and traditional community. By means of their translated writings and the infusion of their attitudes and grievances into American professional psychology in the 1930s and into pop social science thereafter, Adorno and his circle made themselves dramatically felt in the New World. (Since this reception was far more enthusiastic than American conservatives would like to believe, one may have to speak here of a natural fit rather than a deception.) In any case, it is hard to recall Adorno at this point in Western political life mostly for his learned essays on Beethoven and Arnold Schoenberg. Would that musicology were all he wrote!

13. THE MARCUSE FACTOR

Modern Age, Spring 2005

One experience as a graduate student at Yale University that left its lasting mark on me came in the spring of 1964, when Herbert Marcuse arrived to teach a course in the history of socialism, in which I quickly enrolled. With his flowing gray hair, aquiline nose, imposingly long figure, and distinguished German accent, Professor Marcuse made an unexpectedly positive impression on me. It may be necessary to explain the reasons. Certainly our political views were not the same. While I belonged to the Yale Party of the Right (despite being a Rockefeller Republican), Marcuse had supported, or so I learned, the Soviet suppression of the Hungarian uprising in 1956. He also lavished praise on Fidel Castro and other Communist despots. He held no brief for Western bourgeois society, not even what was left of it. Most annoyingly, he referred to those who were left-of-center in American politics as "reactionaries" and treated the welfare state as an instrument for desensitizing American consumers to the evils of capitalism.

Despite these quirks, our new professor was bedazzling as a lecturer. He knew an enormous amount about the subjects that interested me: European intellectual history and especially German philosophy. I had grown up knowing German and had dipped into Kant, Hegel, and Schopenhauer years before enrolling in Marcuse's course. He brought up these and also other thinkers, like Pascal, de Maistre, and Proudhon, while quoting long passages in the original languages. As an intellectually curious twenty-three year old auditor, he simply blew me away.

What is more, his background reminded me of my father's family, German-speaking Jews who had fled from the Nazis and spoke English with a similar inflection. At the time I knew Marcuse, he had not yet become the gray eminence of the New Left. He was still a philosophy professor at Brandeis University, who took a train to New Haven once a week, to hold his class at the Yale Graduate Hall.

It was only later, when he had retired from Brandeis and gone to San Diego State as a teacher that he went off the deep end entirely. In his California phase he openly advocated violence and became identified with the black Communist Party activist Angela Davis. Thirty years later when I spoke to the Hegel scholar Stanley Rosen about his one meeting with Marcuse, Rosen remembered exactly the kind of person I knew, a charming Old World academic with a touch of dottiness. Rosen, too, was stunned by what Marcuse did in California and attributed such behavior to the lack of a moral center, a problem that Rosen had explored in a critical study of Martin Heidegger.

As a graduate student I had not only not perceived such a problem but also found ways of rationalizing Marcuse's defects, almost turning them into excesses of virtue. His outbursts against capitalist one-dimensionality and the corresponding indulgence of Communist mass murder could be attributable to his *ancien régime* elegance and to his genuine shock over American consumerist habits. For the most part, however, I tried not to think about his wicked opinions, because there was no possibility of reconciling them with my own fierce anti-Communism.

Even less did I care for the fantasy that Marcuse had inserted into *Eros and Civilization* (1955) about a fusion of Marx and Freud that would take place in a future socialist world practicing polymorphic sexuality. Although these themes were already present in his contributions to German journals in the 1930s, Marcuse's erotic fixation was not what drew me to him philosophically or socially. Given my up-tight Central European bourgeois upbringing, I simply could not envisage the forbidden pleasures that Marcuse hoped to make available by slaying the capitalist monster. And though he had published a thick volume on Soviet Communism in 1958, which was sympathetically critical of his subject, it was hard for me to imagine that he or anyone else really believed that Stalin was enabling his Russian subjects to enjoy sensual pleasures. Or that the Soviets were featuring more of such pleasures than "repressed" consumers could pick up in Times Square.

As I later figured out, Marcuse leaned toward the Soviets for the same reason he conceived of Western capitalist countries as sexually repressive. Like other members of the Frankfurt School — most notably Theodor Adorno, with whom he had been associated since the early 1930s — Marcuse claimed to detest bourgeois civilization and supposedly wished to see it destroyed.

Still, his connection to what he professed to despise was ambivalent and — like other members of the Frankfurt School, as noted by Lorenz Jäger in his biography of Adorno — Marcuse was in some ways himself an *haute bourgeoisie* anachronism. This was true from the way he dressed to the gallant (but never lecherous) manner in which he spoke to female students. He oozed traditional German *Bildung*, with his extensive humanistic and linguistic erudition, which seemed to contrast sharply with the careerism and the narrow specialization that prevailed among his American counterparts.

He was also far more tolerant of dissenting opinions from his students than my other professors. When I had criticized Woodrow Wilson and his messianic politics in other classes, the instructors had reacted with extreme displeasure. I felt forced to cut off my remarks lest I injure my professional future by expressing unseasonable views (something I ultimately did anyhow). In Marcuse's class, it was different. Unlike my Cold War liberal professors and my current politically correct colleagues, this graying German radical thrived on debate. When he asked that a student argue against Karl Marx's interpretation of the Paris uprising of May 1848, an event that has been seen as an early expression of French working-class consciousness, I volunteered. My presentation, which I pulled mostly out of Alexis de Tocqueville's recollections, evoked a powerful reaction from my Marxist adversary. But as soon as the give-and-take was over, he profusely thanked me for my "valorous efforts" and, perhaps to underline his magnanimity, gave me the highest grade for the course. I was put in mind of this generous spirit many times afterwards, and am still embarrassed to admit that I learned the example of true liberal intellectual exchange from a declared Marxist-Leninist.

Leftist *émigré* social historians have been partly right to stress the rejection experienced by the German-Jewish bourgeoisie in the early twentieth century, in an Austro-German society that viewed them generally as outsiders. Although Jews in Germany succeeded in the professions and even in politics at a much higher rate than elsewhere, possibly including the United States, there was nonetheless an anti-Semitic legacy that made German Jews despair about full acceptance into society, even before the Nazis' accession to power.

Some educated, wealthy German Jews turned toward the cultural and aesthetic Right, as exemplified by the rarefied circle around the poet-seer Stefan George (1868-1933). Despite George's reactionary positions, illustrated by his contempt for modernity and his invocation of a "Third Reich" led by spiritual ascetics and artistic purifiers, well over half of his inner circle was Jewish. German literary commentator Geret Luhr has shown in *Ästhetische Kritik der Moderne* that George's Jewish disciples spanned the political spectrum, from culturally conservative Teutonophile Friedrich Gundolf to Zionist Eric Kahler to Marxist Walter Benjamin. What united this group, however, was an experience of estrangement. They did not fit into the commercial world of their parents any better than into a German society that would continue to keep them at arm's length.

One is in fact struck by the frequency with which such souls contemplated and in some cases committed suicide. George incarnated, albeit for different reasons, a similar alienation and happily accepted the flatteries of young Jews, even suggesting in an oft-quoted poem in *Stern des Bundes* that he was mediating artistically between "the swarthy and blond brothers who had sprung from the same womb but do not recognize each other, and therefore wander forever, without being fulfilled." (The reader is asked to put up with this translation of a difficult but brilliant poet.) Were I alive at the time, I too in all likelihood would have been a *George-Anhänger*.

But another reaction that arose among snubbed German-Jewish bourgeois was an anti-national, anti-bourgeois stance that easily morphed into reckless social radicalism. While the forms taken by this reaction have not been particularly salutary, for many years I hoped to separate the fruits from their bitter source. In my once-held view, those who had tried to expose the corruptness and oppressive condition of pre-socialist Western life were exaggerating middle-class, capitalist malevolence because of the circumstances of their youth and because of their perpetual search for a "fascist" enemy after their experience with the Nazis. Nonetheless, I persisted in thinking that it was possible to extract from this trauma a core of methodological truth. Despite their derailments, Marcuse and his friends did carry with them a usable form of social analysis, a philosophy of history, and an awareness of the ideological dimension of political life: all of which Anglo-American society was ignoring or obdurately refusing to incorporate into self-studies. I had arrived at this view after studying under Marcuse and coming to respect his learning.

I was also outraged that the Yale graduate school would not offer him a chair in the history of socialism and Marxism after his expected retirement from Brandeis. Having voted in the fall (reluctantly) for Goldwater for president, I found it hypocritical to condemn my professors for right-wing bigotry. But when a classmate began to condemn the anti-Marcuseites as "liberal fascists," I decided to adopt that term. I could thereby attack my professors, who were mostly Kennedy-Johnson Democrats, without having to move toward the Left and while continuing to support my teacher, who by then was heading west.

What might have put him over the edge on the West Coast, I have long believed, were the unwillingness of Brandeis to extend his contract (beyond the retirement age) and the refusal of Yale to establish a position for this distinguished thinker. When Marcuse on a visit to Venice told the mayor that there were too many tasteless people swarming around and that "*si ha bisogno qua d'un turismo di qualità*," unlike Alasdair MacIntyre, who reported this incident with extreme irritation, I was amused rather than offended. Just because Marcuse held unsavory opinions about some things, I thought, did not require him to accept the soiling and improper use of architectural treasures.

The last time I came to his defense was in 1979, after he died and *National Review* had published an abrasive obituary. At that time I submitted to the magazine an impassioned retort, noting Marcuse's contribution to Hegel studies in *Reason and Revolution*. *National Review* never published this endorsement of a famous radical coming from a conservative scholar. My gesture might have created even more cognitive dissonance than the lifelong tendency of Sidney Hook, a fiercely anti-Communist social democrat, to say nice things about Marx. Even then I was to the right of Hook politically, while Marcuse and the Frankfurt School were culturally far more radical than the father of Communism.

My interest in Marcuse in any case led me into reading Adorno and Adorno's collaborator Max Horkheimer and by the late 1980s into becoming associated with *Telos*, a journal that had been founded to popularize in the United States the Critical Theory of the Frankfurt School. Under its editor-in-chief Paul Piccone, *Telos* moved generally rightward starting in the mid-1980s; nonetheless, my colleague Wesley

McDonald expressed horror that I took up with these "weird people" who would not likely participate in an ISI seminar.

Despite such objections, I was comfortable in my new company, and as my neoconservative adversaries took over leadership positions on the American Right, I found a justification to shift camps. My new comrades were graying New Leftists who had moved away from specifically leftist Frankfurt School positions. By then they were supplementing their changing belief systems or investigative methodologies by adding ideas from Carl Schmitt and other European critics of liberalism. In issue after issue one learned how the radical god had failed — though not in some dramatic fashion as that story unfolds in the contributions to the book bearing that title. There was, however, one problem I soon learned. Wherever my fellow-editors happened to be looking for ideas, including the humanism of Irving Babbitt, they kept returning to the Frankfurt School.

By the early 1990s I had tired of this cult and of the mechanical hero worship it engendered. There were in fact Frankfurt School texts that I found instructive, particularly *Dialectic of the Enlightenment* and *Negative Dialectics*, both of which analyze social and cultural phenomena in a manner that I as a non-leftist could appreciate. Adorno's attacks on bureaucratic structures and on Enlightened rationalism, a theme that runs through *Dialectic of the Enlightenment*, has profoundly conservative implications — provided one can separate such perceptions from the muddled syntax and provided one can read through the intertwined feminist mythology. One should be free, I thought, to take from Adorno, Horkheimer, and Marcuse what seems relevant and to dump the rest.

One should also be encouraged to criticize the defects in their interpretive tradition. Not everything that came out of their activity, I explained, has to be considered good. But those opinions did not prevail in the *Telos* circle. Thus, a work as long and influential as *The Authoritarian Personality*, which Adorno, Horkheimer, and other Frankfurt School members constructed during and after the Second World War, was declared to be atypical of its creators. According to the received doctrine, its purpose was to generate cash for the exiled authors, who never did anything faintly resembling this study again. The obsession there with "fascist personalities" and the attempt to uncover such types among white Christian heterosexuals in the United States was supposedly a wartime aberration.

But even a cursory reading of Rolf Wiggershaus's authoritative German study of the Frankfurt School proves the opposite: namely, that one finds similar work done by the usual suspects well before *The Authoritarian Personality*, going back to Frankfurt in the 1930s, and there is evidence of Adorno pursuing the same subjects after his return to Germany in 1950. But it was impossible to bring this up to my collaborators without causing noisy, offended denial.

It was also difficult to present to my usually amiable colleagues in New York the (to me) self-evident truth that much of the radical project of the Frankfurt School was attributable to the Jewishness of its founders. Without their sense of marginalization and the attendant hostilities, they would not likely have been so contemptuous of ordinary, non-adjusted bourgeois. This was particularly true of Adorno, despite his Catholic upbringing and his French mother, whose maiden name he took, and despite the fact that his Jewish father shared none of his hang-ups. A Hungarian Jewish social theorist, Ferenc Feher, who had written for *Telos*, made this point exhaustively in a book I eventually read. Although Feher was clearly on to something and heavily documented his contentions, my friends went on condemning "his ridiculous nonsense."

When I defended Feher's interpretation in an essay for the journal, they turned on me with impatience. Their editorial judgment suggested that I was recycling a position that is intrinsically anti-Semitic. The inconsistency I saw in this opinion was for me as maddening as the selective victimology of the Euro-American multiculturalists. How can one pretend to be looking at the social and existential ground of politics but refuse to apply this method to those who turn it against their adversaries? No matter what they claimed about themselves as "free-floating intellectuals" (*freischwebende Intelligenz*), the members of the Frankfurt School were as influenced by their backgrounds and the baggage it brought as those they excoriated.

It was my deepening friendship with Piccone, who died in 2004, and with his faithful companion Gary Ulmen, the onetime assistant of Karl Wittfogel, that kept me in the *Telos* circle long after my fondness for the Frankfurt School had dried up. Piccone, Ulmen, the political theorist George Schwab, and I became fast friends and co-workers on various projects relating to Carl Schmitt. My interest in Schmitt superseded my predilection for Critical Theory, but since the two remained connected with the same group and publication, I never revealed to

Piccone or Ulmen my change of heart. I had no further desire to tackle the job of "salvaging something" from the Frankfurt School so as to pass that something on to a younger generation.

True, *Telos* did sometimes feature themes that questioned the relevance of Critical Theory in a self-liquidating bourgeois society; nonetheless, most of the contributors clung stubbornly to the old faith, even while denying it. When the political uses began to look *passé*, some took to writing about Adorno's defense and composition of atonal music, as a revolt against bourgeois conformity. By then I felt even further out of the loop, seeing that I found Adorno's musical compositions unbearable to listen to. Would that everyone practiced fascist conformity by listening to Mozart and Vivaldi!

Indeed trying to preserve a living Critical Theory was coming to resemble the play-acting of contemporary European Marxism. Yuppies who plunge into every politically correct fad in France and Germany pretend to be Marxists broadly understood. By carefully cherry-picking Marx's collected works, they can depict a master who is forever fashionable, whether as an ecologist, an advocate of open borders, or someone who would have championed homosexual marriage. Among my liberal Christian colleagues all the same attributes are heaped onto Jesus, by reducing the New Testament to two or three overworked or deconstructed verses. An honest disciple would abandon a master whose teachings he can no longer accept, before twisting his words into pretzels.

Much has happened to me and to others since I first entered Herbert Marcuse's class. My teacher died after his less than dignified golden years, and my colleagues from *Telos* have either passed on into the *molestam senectutis* or into what awaits at the end of the aging process. To think of myself now as a disciple of Marcuse or of the broader Frankfurt School movement to which he belonged has become difficult but not impossible. I remain a *Telos* editor, and following the tragic death of our ebullient chief editor, we were scheduled to meet early in 2005 to discuss the publication's future. (It has already been decided that it will have a tomorrow.) In provocative reviews of my last two books, the analytic philosopher David Gordon has portrayed me as a right-wing exponent of the Frankfurt School. I am what Adorno or Marcuse would have been if they had been bourgeois conservatives, applying their critical method to leftist targets.

This image amuses me, but overlooks certain elementary distinctions that Gordon understands better than I. You cannot be a Critical Theorist unless you share the corresponding world view. A social analyst may adapt Adorno or the Italian Marxist Antonio Gramsci while pursuing diametrically opposed moral and cultural ends. But the effect is not to replicate the same body of thought while transposing it to a different ideological location. To provide a case in point: a conservative may notice the applicability of Critical method for exposing leftist power structures. But the result of applying it is not what the social theorists who fashioned this method intended it to do.

There is an intention in political theory, unlike say technology, that is inseparable from a particular form of inquiry. No one in his right mind would confuse "right-wing Gramscians," who emphasize the hegemonic ideologies of the Left, with the dominant ideas of the Italian Communist Party, which also idolized Gramsci. Context counts in examining the relation of social and political thinkers to each other. And no matter how respectfully men of the Right, like Samuel Francis or Alain de Benoist, speak about Gramsci as a methodological teacher, there is a difference between an adaptable idea and the political persuasion to which it pertains.

I am making this point to underline my reservations about describing myself as an Adornoite or a Marcuseite simply because I have borrowed from the interwar Left a particular strategy for unmasking contemporary leftists. Such borrowing is different from membership in the tradition whose ideas one is adapting. Those Federalists who framed the Judicial Act of 1789 were not the precursors of today's judicial activists, even though both may have favored a powerful judiciary controlling state legislatures. One group of judicial activists was trying to hold back mass democracy; the other group, by contrast, wishes to push it in a more radical direction than legislatures are likely to go. Intention is integral to our understanding of social and political positions.

What may be argued, however, is that intellectual traditions bind people in spite of their obvious differences. Thus, Pierre Manent, in his anthology of liberal theorists and in his *Histoire Intellectuelle du Libéralisme*, links figures who would not likely have agreed on the best form of government but who nonetheless contributed to a recognizable liberal tradition of thought. While Machiavelli, Rousseau, Hobbes, and Montesquieu would not have all rallied to popular government or the ideal of social equality, according to Manent, they did represent stages in the development of a coherent and identifiably liberal world view. One encounters themes or undercurrents in their work — for example the disentanglement of political life from ecclesiastical authority, a constructivist notion of government, human nature identified with the individual will inventing what human beings are, and a separation of state and society — that define a "liberal" post-medieval school of thought.

Without embracing his intellectualist approach entirely, it seems to me that Manent is correct to underscore the possibility of a far-ranging agreement about certain premises among thinkers who would not otherwise have much in common. Thus, he treats side-by-side Montesquieu and Rousseau, because of shared views about the artificiality of government, the association of commercial life with a softening of manners, and general skepticism about Christianity. This same approach might also indicate that right-wing and left-wing Critical Theorists hold common assumptions, for example about the determinative character of class and history and about the centrality of power in the promotion of modern ideologies, despite their evident divergences.

Thus, I may still be partly on Marcuse's side, when it comes to interpreting political behavior. In the war between nature and history, I still generally come down among those who stress historical contexts and power relations. While Marcuse may not have been the only thinker who espoused this perspective, he played a key role in presenting it to me. That I later rediscovered this perspective in genuinely conservative and even counterrevolutionary writers is not surprising. By then I had developed a strong distaste for Marcuse's political teachings and exhibitionism and (perhaps) tried to find other exponents for ideas I had picked up initially from this *maître à penser*.

But there may be more to this memory from the distant past, which has often merged in my mind with my encounter with Marcuse. About the time I was taking his class, I began reading certain authors who became critical for my later thinking. Two texts that Marcuse brought up in class often enough to get me to read them were de Maistre's *Soirées* and Hegel's *Philosophy of Right.* The attempts by both authors, one from a Catholic counterrevolutionary background and the other from a conservative liberal position, to understand the impact of history on human nature made a powerful impression on me as a graduate student. Significantly, not until I read these continental authors did I reach for Burke's *Reflections*, which I still find the most compelling presentation of a historically based conservatism. Burke's perceptions about the moral value of habituation, the social, hierarchical preconditions for virtue, and his defense of historical continuities seemed all the more impressive because Burke was upholding a then still traditional society. It was also not a static one but open to piecemeal reform.

At the same time, I found in the Yale Sterling Library the original German edition, written during the rise of Nazism, of Eric Voegelin's *Political Religions*. There are few books that have imprinted my scholarship more than this text, and since my late twenties, I have steadily applied Voegelin's insights about the mythical paradigms mixed into modern ideologies. This influence came, moreover, after I had studied ancient Greek and became deeply absorbed in the craft and the fatalism of Thucydides. In my case there was an ancient as well as a modern template against which I tried to understand historical patterns and political motives. It is altogether possible that my longtime preoccupation with the snares of power, symbolized for Thucydides by Ate, the goddess of mischief, came from the *Histories* as much as from Marcuse. Looking back on these sources and inspirations, it is hard to single out any one figure as my preferred thinker.

What Marcuse certainly did provide was intellectual stimulation and a pedagogical model at a time when I needed both. He was a doorway to other, more profound learning, but he could not move beyond his role for reasons explained in a passage that I gave my students to translate from Plato's *Criton*. "*Epeide he nosos enepipte kai diephtheire ten polin, poi eistha su, poteron pros tous philous oupros ton iatron?*" [If a plague befell and devastated the city to whom would you turn, your friends or the doctor?] Criton's answer is "*Pros ton iatron ea — san de entautha kai philoi. Edei gar ho iatros ta peri tes nosou, empeiroteros on - ehoi alloi.*" [Naturally I would go to the doctor, where I would find my friends. For the doctor would know about illness, being more knowledgeable than the others.] Herbert Marcuse offered *philia* rather than *iatrikon*, which may be the reason that our relation could not develop beyond the point it did. He was an older companion, but he could not treat the illness of the soul nor explain the human condition more fully than what he taught me at the age of twenty-three.

14. MUSSOLINI IN THE MIDEAST

The American Conservative, July 2005

Reading a blast on David Horowitz's *FrontPage Magazine* against journalist Eric Margolis for his "apologizing for Islamo-fascists," I was reminded of George Orwell's observation about his fellow leftists in 1946: "The word fascism has now no meaning except in so far as it signifies 'something not desirable.'"

In an endorsement of Daniel Pipes, who was then a candidate for membership in the U.S. Institute of Peace, *FrontPage Magazine* praised him as someone who had "perhaps done more than anyone else to clear up the confusion and obfuscation about the threat to our nation from the forces of radical Islamofascism." Significantly, Pipes, who publishes widely on "militant Islam," usually avoids the term "Islamofascism" in his work. After all, it is possible to criticize Islamic fundamentalism and the failure of Europeans to adjust their immigration policy to fit this danger without bringing up Hitler and Mussolini.

That, however, is not how others see this matter. In *Terror and Liberalism*, Paul Berman equates fascism with hatred for beleaguered minorities — "the subversive dwellers in Babylon" allied to Satanic forces. It is the paranoid reaction of those who believe "the Satanic forces were always pressing the people of God from all sides." "Yet, no matter how putrid and oppressive was the present, the reign of God always beckoned in the future."

For Christopher Hitchens, the "bombers of Manhattan represent fascism with an Islamic face .... What they abominate about 'the West,' to put it in a phrase, is not what Western liberals don't like and can't defend about their own system but what they *do* like about it and must defend: its emancipated women, its scientific inquiry, its separation of religion from the state." Hitchens deems the essence of fascism, which militant Muslims now incarnate, to be hatred of "the very idea of modernity and the related practices of pluralism and toleration."

Such assertions need to be questioned. Hitchens's "modernity," for example, only refers to the most recent phase of Western modernity, a process of change that starts with the Protestant Reformation, various religious wars, and the age of absolutism. It is also doubtful, if one looks at the rigorous enforcement of political correctness, that we are now living in a time of unprecedented tolerance. One might wonder whether the attempt to drive religion out of public life, a practice that Hitchens proudly endorses, exemplifies toleration or social engineering. Finally, there are competing visions of modernity, not all of which exclude religious piety and traditional gender roles. Hitchens fixes on his preferred notion of modernity, which he makes synonymous with the West.

Critics of Islamofascism never quite succeed in relating their *bête noire* to a historically recognizable interwar movement. A characteristically vague definition crops up in an interview conducted by Jamie Glazov in *FrontPage Magazine* with Stephen Vincent, the author of a book on Iraqi society who is made out to be an expert on the new fascism. Vincent talks up those Iraqis epitomizing "the feminine spirit" and "the rejection of tribal culture" but then expresses concern that the wrong kinds of people may take over in Iraq. "Islamofascists declare that they 'love death more than we love life.' In truth, they are enraptured by a kind of malignant narcissism exacerbated by the grandiosity that lurks at the heart of Islam." Further, "Nazis, Communist revolutionaries, Islamofascists are warriors and terrorists. All believe in their superhuman will to transcend the ego and to possess the Infinite." Although those terrorists Vincent depicts may be a nasty bunch, it is not clear what makes them fascist — as opposed to merely unpleasant. What link do they have to the Italian war veterans who marched on Rome in 1922 and brought Mussolini to power — or to the Brown Shirts of Ernst Roehm?

Some anti-Islamofascists relate their object of attack to anti-Jewish propaganda and to a rejection of liberalism. One problem with pairing dislike for liberalism with recrudescent fascism is the need for agreement on the meanings of both terms. Some of us may find Hitchens's liberalism to be downright illiberal, and although European fascists denounced them as decadent bourgeois, most European liberals held traditional views on women and gays that Berman and Hitchens might consider to be fascist.

Even more problematic, not all fascists were violently anti-Semitic or sympathized with Hitler's treatment of European Jewry. The head of the Spanish Falange, a group of Spanish nationalists whom Berman goes after, deplored Nazi anti-Semitism and drew sharp contrasts between Christianity and Aryan racism. Moreover, until the late 1930s, about a tenth of Italian Jews held *tessere del partito*, as fascists in good standing. The passage by Mussolini of anti-Jewish legislation in 1938, after he threw in his lot with Hitler, shocked European and American Jewish leaders, who at that time viewed the *Duce* as an ally against Nazi Germany and a reliable supporter of the Zionists.

It is also not clear that fascists, despite their passion for military strutting, did much to change the status of women in European societies. Women held party offices and continued to vote in fascist-led countries in which female suffrage had been granted. And even "clerical-fascist" Austria in the 1930s did not drive women from public life or show anything like the ugly face one finds in Islamist societies. If the real European experiments in clerical fascism in interwar Austria and Portugal were what our critics are looking at, it is hard to see why they should be offended or even care about clerical fascism among Muslims.

But that kind of genealogical investigation is not what is taking place. What anti-fascist critics are doing is conflating everything they consider "not desirable" into a single threat against which Western governments are to be mobilized. This hypothetical force is seen as antithetical to what the critics happen to value, in Hitchens's case secularism and feminism.

Although sometimes attempts at historical connections between Islamofascism and the real article are made, the lines of continuity are less than convincing. For Stephen Schwartz in *The Two Faces of Islam*, an aberrant strain of Islam, Wahhabism, established itself in the Arabian Peninsula in the eighteenth century, whereupon it created a theocracy, which the Saud rulers dedicated themselves to keeping in place and which over time, we are made to believe, came to resemble European fascism. As the Wahhabi movement, which prescribes tight behavioral control in a polity under Islamic law, spread into other parts of the Islamic world, it helped forge an anti-Western front that is still with us. Because of its authoritarian and anti-Jewish character, this Islamist front is now, according to Schwartz, a major world danger. It encourages a fascist mentality that is similar to the one that imperiled Western liberal democracy in interwar Europe.

Schwartz, whom Hitchens considers "a most articulate enemy of Islamofascism," has tried to publicize his take on the "West and fascism" as a newswriter for Voice of America and as a frequent speaker at the Heritage Foundation and American Enterprise Institute. Critics of Islamofascism have come up with other apparently damning links between Islamists and European fascism. They cite the support of the Grand Mufti of Jerusalem, an implacable opponent of the Zionists, for Nazi Germany in World War II and the prominence of Muslims in the Croatian nationalist government, the Ustasha, which served Nazi Germany. Such critics might also note (but they don't for PC reasons) that Muslim Albanians formed an entire unit of the Waffen-SS and under German command happily slaughtered Serbs. But such facts have nothing to do with militant Islam. The Muslims who worked for the Nazis in the Balkans were mostly secularized, and the Grand Mufti sought Nazi aid as a crazed anti-Zionist rather than because he saw a fit between the Koran and Aryan racism. The Hashemite monarchies in Iraq and Jordan and the Saud dynasty in Arabia all eventually took sides with the Allies in World War II.

It is possible to condemn such behavior as stoning women for talking to men on the street without attaching a fascist label. Medieval crusaders sacked Jews and Eastern Christians *en route* to the Middle East but not because the crusaders were fascists. And it is morally and politically justifiable to keep hostile Third World populations away from one's country, whether or not they qualify as fascists. David Horowitz properly warns the Dutch about the havoc being wrought on their society by Third World Muslim immigrants. But he adds nothing substantive here by condemning the recently arrived Muslims as Islamofascists.

There are two reasons for the current inflation of the meaning of "fascist" to take in anti-Western, anti-Israeli, and generally unprogressive Muslims, but both involve faulty historical parallels.

First, among left-liberals in the U.S. but even more in Europe, anti-fascism rules. Fascists are the opposite of what the Left considers good, be it gay marriage, open borders, or the view that gender is a social construct. Part of this demonology consists of defending Communists or at least savaging anti-Communists of the past. But Communists in practice rarely supported the expressive freedoms that anti-fascists are calling for — any more than did the real fascists. The Communist parties in Western Europe viewed unconventional social morality with deep suspicion. Just ask gays there (if one can find them outside of prison) about life in Castro's Cuba or Communist China.

Anti-fascism is a ritual activity that consists of anathematizing those who do not share the fashionable social agenda by linking them to long dead anti-Communist tyrants. Hitchens's invectives against "fascism with an Islamic face" and against "theocratic barbarism" illustrate this style of thinking. The enemies are "not fighting to free Gaza. They are fighting for the right to throw acid in the faces of unveiled women in Kabul and Karachi." Thus Hitchens explains fascist misogyny to readers of the London *Evening Standard* in the week following 9/11. His fevered phraseology is intended to remind us of a danger that is both theocratic and anti-feminist. Although it is proper to condemn barbaric conduct, it may be asked whether all non-secular societies are necessarily barbaric and whether what Hitchens is describing is specifically fascist.

Clearly, some who rail against Islamofascism, like Hitchens and Peter Beinart and Andrew Sullivan of *The New Republic*, have domestic fish to fry. They all see the possibility of tying together the war against Islamic theocratic fascists abroad with one against the hated Religious Right at home. As Murray Rothbard once noted about John Dewey and the circle grouped around *The New Republic* that agitated for American entry into World War I, plunging one's country into foreign crusades has often been a means for changing things at home. The enemies of Islamofascism are not the first to play this game.

Second, the more widespread cause for the agitation against Islamofascism is the advancement of a particular Middle Eastern agenda. It is not surprising that anti-Islamofascists are often neoconservatives. One can look all day at Democratic leftist websites without chancing upon a single reference to Islamofascists. But this is not true for the commentaries of Sean Hannity, Michael Savage, Charles Krauthammer, Mort Kondracke, *FrontPage Magazine*, or the websites of *The New Republic* and *National Review* or the neocon fellow traveler Andrew Sullivan. All of them bristle with denunciations of the new fascism. For neoconservatives, like the Left, fascism is a word to conjure with. It is usually made to refer to anti-Semitism, Hitler, and his genocidal politics — themes that elicit powerful emotions.

But it would be unfair to treat this fascist connection as merely cynical manipulation. Neoconservatives who bring it up may well believe that they face an encircling fascist, anti-Semitic enemy. For example, it is hard to read the immaculately neoconservative *New York Post* even for a week without encountering terrified accounts of prowling neo-Nazis in Europe.

It is doubtful that neoconservatives are entirely ignorant of the struggle that is now taking place over the manipulation of the fascist label. And they are weighing into this battle by trying to popularize their own hyphenated fascist entry. This may be the most important explanation for why Islamofascism is now thriving in certain quarters. And the term may stay around as long as the semantic battle continues to unfold.

15. ROGUE NOTIONS

The American Conservative, June 2008

It would be wrong to imagine that while Republicans are driven by their desire to transform those who are not like us politically and culturally, their Democratic opposition holds radically different premises. Both national parties, and even two publications with such supposedly opposing worldviews as *National Review* and *The New Republic,* engage in the same Wilsonian rhetoric, and both sides of the political center view foreign countries as places for trying out our progressive ideals. Both use the language of human rights, and both believe that if the U.S. is to be true to itself, it must export its values as a foreign-policy priority.

The values that we are urged to export, moreover, are coterminous with how democracy evolved in twentieth-century society, with special emphasis on the treatment of women, minorities, and on a certain acquisitive individualism identified with the opening of markets and a mixed economy.

Where the center Left and center Right differ is in how much energy they would expend on such a world democratic mission and whether they would pursue their idealistic goals unilaterally or with other powers. Historian John Ehrmann in *The Rise of the Neoconservatives* makes the telling observation that during the Clinton administration, the architects of our present Republican foreign policy were generally upset by the lack of resolve in the president's handling of international relations. But these critics were pleased that Clinton and his foreign policy team raised democratic ideals in public forums. And they mostly did not dissent in 1999, when Clinton provided impeccably Wilsonian reasons for bombing Serb forces in Kosovo. That act was justified as an expression of our commitment to human rights and to the fashioning of a pluralistic society in Kosovo.

There is, of course, no justification for thinking, like Bill Clinton and George W. Bush, that all of mankind yearns for the current brand of American democracy. Nonetheless, those who hold this position have advantages over their critics. They belong to the boards of influential magazines and prestigious Beltway institutes. They are therefore more likely to get their views and biases accepted as policy than those who are kept out of the public discussion. Moreover, the manner in which American history is now presented in public education and the media glorifies powerful and expanded executive government. The presidents whom educators, popular historians, and journalists place in their pantheon have combined strong economic control with grand military crusades for globalist, egalitarian ideals.

While this precedent has certainly not helped to deflect criticism from Bush's crusade in Iraq for secularism and women's rights, as well as against terrorism, certain critical factors must be looked at to explain the president's lack of popularity, particularly on the Left. He is a Republican and therefore the representative of what is considered a right-wing party, teeming with Evangelicals and other undesirables whom proper liberal intellectuals are supposed to despise. And the war is a big deal for the declared enemies of the Democrats, who condemn them on Fox and talk radio as the "unpatriotic Left."

But one should recognize these rhetorical outbursts for what they are: expressions of narrow partisanship. They do not prove that the only course that is consistent with Democratic thinking is shamefaced, blame-America retreat from international affairs. Nor does the center Left necessarily view wars intended to spread democracy as extrinsic to its own traditions. Vigorous presidents, who steamrolled everything in their way to launch crusades against reactionary forces at home and abroad, furnish the hagiography of the Democratic Party. In this respect — though no other — I find myself agreeing with Senator Joe Lieberman and the editorial board of *The New Republic* when they remind us of their party's history. A party that still exalts Wilson, FDR, Kennedy, and Truman as its great presidents is not destined to become a permanent gathering of non-interventionists. An Obama administration might be less interested in internationalist crusades than Bush has been but only because it would be more concerned with feminist or minority programs and income redistribution. That is different from saying that Democrats do not embrace a religion of global democracy. Democrats express the same impulse as their Republican opposition toward making others more like us, as a look at the speeches of Bill

Clinton and Madeleine Albright during and after their adventure in Kosovo strongly suggests.

Those who favor liberal internationalist policies have cobbled together arguments or assertions that have flourished in public discourse. Although mostly based on hyperbole and flawed historical parallels, these opinions have gained considerable ground through being featured in widely circulated journals, the national press, and among the political class generally.

First, they hold that it is immoral or inconsistent to claim that democracy is good for one's own people without trying to bestow it on everyone else. Here one finds embedded certain long familiar themes that still resonate, especially Christian universalism, the Kantian categorical imperative, and disembodied phrases taken from the Declaration of Independence about natural and presumably globally extendible rights. Although these themes usually do not amount to a cohesive argument, they do constitute a rhetorically effective explanation for why others should pay us the flattery of imitation.

But what can we do if others do not relish our goodies, despite the fact that, according to Bush and *The Weekly Standard*, every man in the world — provided he knows what is good for him — hungers for our brand of freedom? Alas, there is no convincing evidence that everyone in the world wants our democracy, even if we can reasonably assume that Pakistani women have no desire to be put to death as fornicators after being raped. Pointing out that some people find certain local practices repugnant is different from demonstrating that traditional societies are eager to follow us politically and culturally. Asserting that most people would like to avoid suffering is not the same as demonstrating that they would like to incorporate the features of our late modern society, starting with secularism, an atomistic society, children liberated from parental control, a right to abortions, and the open exhibition of gay lifestyles.

As for the naturalness of what we desire for others, one is reminded of David Hume's challenge to John Locke's assertions that civil societies arose out of a state of nature in order to protect a universally demanded list of natural rights. In *Of the Original Contract*, Hume noted that the form of consensual government that Locke saw as natural to the human condition had nothing to do with "the common sentiment of mankind" or the "practice and opinion of all nations and all ages." Wrote Hume, "what authority any moral reasoning can have, which leads into opinions so wide of the general practice of mankind, in every place but this single kingdom, it is easy to determine." Although Hume believed that "in the speculative sciences" an "appeal to general opinion" might be "deemed unfair and inconclusive," in examining moral and cultural values there is "no other standard by which any controversy can be decided." What Locke considered a universal right, "that citizens must consent to being taxed," is certainly an honorable position for an English Whig, but does not seem to be something that most people would view as a foundation of civil government.

What Hume points to as an overgeneralization should apply to liberal internationalists as well: they should be able to cite more illustrations of what they think is natural. Equally important, the view that it was necessary, or so the neoconservatives argue, to bomb the Germans and Japanese back into the Stone Age to give them what Allan Bloom approvingly calls "an educational experience" makes one wonder why mass destruction should be required to teach people what they should want.

The second set of arguments activated by liberal internationalists centers on the proposition that unless we work to save souls for democracy, we will have a world perpetually at war. Only democracies, according to every neoconservative scribbler on this planet, can be peaceful. Indeed, non-democratic governments are compulsively mischievous and will, unless brought to see the light, unleash war on the bearers of democratic virtue. This argument has historical and conceptual defects, though it is proclaimed so often and so loudly by those in power that most intellectuals take its merit for granted. Typically its advocates construct a Manichean scheme running throughout human history, or at least as far back as the ancient Athenians, in which the democratic and anti-democratic sides are always pitted against each other. But until the very modern era, it is sometimes difficult to tell the democracies from the non-democracies.

Consider slaveholding Athens under Cleisthenes, in which women were subject to total male control and less than ten percent of the residents were enfranchised, as opposed to military-aristocratic Sparta, where, according to Aristotle, women held vast financial power and there was a wide electorate of "equals." It would not be amiss to point out that "liberal democracy," which our internationalists idolize, is a very recent product of a later modern civilization. The egalitarian attitudes extending even to gender relations, the role of public

administration, the operation of secularizing tendencies, and the presence of large urban concentrations are all of decisive importance to
understand this historical configuration. It is certainly not the most
recent manifestation of the Athenian *polis* or of eighteenth-century
British Whig politics.

Despite the need for such perspective, neoconservative classicists
Donald Kagan and Victor Davis Hanson have spilled rivulets of ink
explaining how the struggle between Athens and Sparta, or "democratic" Thebes and proto-fascist Sparta, foreshadowed certain modern
confrontations, for example, between the democratic Union under
Lincoln's benevolent leadership and the slavo-cratic Confederacy, or
the global democrats Wilson and Churchill versus the demonic Kaiser
Bill. Such anachronistic comparisons always seem to involve the same
legerdemain, turning whatever side the writer hates into a precursor
of the Nazis (whence the inescapable *argumentum ad Hitlerum*) and
making the righteous victory appear counterfactually as a step towards
the latest super-duper version of U.S. democracy.

But things become dodgy when advocates of the world democratic
peace offer conceptual proofs. The term "democracy" is applied to
some societies but not others, depending on whom the author does
or does not like. Societies that in the past bore some degree of family
resemblance to each other socially and even politically — England,
Austria, and Germany in 1914 — have their typological differences
overstated, while those societies that the author favors are declared to
be approximations of present American democracy. Also conveniently
disregarded in defining "liberal" and "democratic" is the thoroughly
illiberal way in which "democratic" societies have acted in war. Is it
really possible, for example, to show that Germany and Austria dealt
with dissent during World War I more brutally than Wilson's government once it decided to plunge into the European conflict? And
was Churchill's move in the summer of 1914 to impose a blockade
on Germany — in violation of international law — before the guns of
August had fired, any less a breach of good behavior than Germany's
appeal to necessity when it violated Belgian neutrality? Such a violation of Belgian sovereignty, by the way, had been part of Britain's and
France's own war planning in the preceding decade.

A most incisive treatment of this double standard can be found in an
article, "The Myth of the Democratic Peace" by Thomas Schwartz and
Kiron K. Skinner, which appeared in *Orbis*. Particularly noteworthy is

the authors' dissection of Wilson's declaration of war "against Prussian dictatorship," an analysis that leads Schwartz and Skinner to observe that Germany in 1914 was a state under law in which "chancellors who lost parliamentary votes of confidence typically quit." Germany was among the first countries to practice universal male suffrage, while "Britain had a still potent House of Lords and a class-based system of advancement in the civil service and armed forces, and the southern United States had a disenfranchised and terrorized racial minority — actually a majority in Mississippi and South Carolina — and one-party rule." This passage is certainly not intended to demonize the Anglo-American side in the war. It is an attempt, however, to suggest what the other side could have brought up about those qualities that rendered the "democracies" as illiberal as their enemies. Schwartz and Skinner are especially good at revealing the selective treatment of historical data by advocates of the proposition that "democracies never fight each other." Until quite recently, there were few, if any, governments anywhere on earth that would qualify as democracies in the current usage of that term. By modern standards, all regimes were racist, sexist, elitist, and did not grant what are today expected welfare measures — with the exceptions of the German and Austrian governments, which did provide relatively generous workers' benefits. Among this vast array of non-democracies that used to pollute our planet, some behaved peacefully and others did not. It may therefore not be the approval of culturally biased liberal internationalists but some other characteristic that defines which types of governments are desirous of peace and which are not.

And some of the features of modern democracy, particularly democratic messianism and popular nationalism, contribute to a stirring of the international pot. The notion that all countries must be brought — willingly or kicking and screaming — into the democratic fold is an invitation to belligerence. The notion that only democracies such as ours can be peaceful is what Edmund Burke called an "armed doctrine." It is also one that, as Richard Gamble amply shows in *The War for Righteousness*, was associated by theological defenders of Woodrow Wilson and his "crusade for democracy" with expanded American political control and a divine mandate to reform the world. It is simply ridiculous to treat the pursuit of peace based on world democratic conversion as a peaceful enterprise. This is a barely disguised adaptation of the Communist goal of bringing about world harmony through world-wide socialist revolution.

Those who challenge the "democratic peace" are called morally callous. In *The Closing of the American Mind*, Allan Bloom finds moral defects in those who dare to hold different views about American foreign policy. One of his least favorite political thinkers, George Kennan, is scolded as a "relativist" for having tried to remove ideological passions from international relations. According to Bloom, "And when we Americans speak seriously about politics, we mean that our principles of freedom and equality and the rights based on them are rational and everywhere applicable. World War II was really an educational experiment undertaken to force those who do not accept these principles to do so." Apparently it is necessary to dehumanize "anti-democracies," to insist on unconditional surrender, and to ravage civilian populations with firebombs and atomic weapons — an "educational experiment" that had to be brought to completion.

Surely we can find less vindictive and less pedagogical ways to deal with security problems or with the occasional need to remove a destructive tyranny. My model here would be the successful effort of British Tories in the early nineteenth century to rid the world of the slave trade, something they accomplished without trying to transmit British parliamentary monarchy to other parts of the globe.

There are times when force is necessary to deal with physical threats to one's country, but it can be carried out without setting ideologues loose on the land. Such meddlers are not particularly helpful in resolving conflict and are more likely to inject into difficult situations an element of moral fanaticism. Unfortunately, with their grip on both sides of the political divide so sure, it's unlikely these would-be educators will be brought under control in the foreseeable future.

16. INVISIBLE FIST

The American Conservative, October 2008

History was supposed to have ended in 1989 with the triumph of Western-style democracy and capitalism. The fall of the Berlin Wall proved, at least to the satisfaction of many American pundits and academics, that economic and political liberty advanced hand in hand. Prosperity must bring freedom and vice versa, a virtuous cycle that would lead the developing world inexorably toward American ideals.

But after 20 years, an alternative scenario has arisen. "By shifting from Communist command economy to capitalism, China and Russia have switched to a far more efficient brand of authoritarianism," Azar Gat of Tel Aviv University argued in *Foreign Affairs*. These countries "could establish a powerful authoritarian-capitalist order that allies political elites, industrialists and the military; that is nationalist in orientation; and that participates in the global economy on its own terms." Indeed, our erstwhile Cold War foes are doing well with their new economic systems. Russia under Putin and China since the end of Maoism have both registered high rates of economic growth. In Russia, disposable income in the last six years has risen almost fourfold, while unemployment has gone down by more than half. There and in China, the vast majority express a high degree of satisfaction with the way the government has handled the economy.

This stands in sharp contrast to public opinion in America, where 82 percent of the population considers the country to be "headed in the wrong direction." As the events of recent weeks have shown, democratic capitalism — once imagined to be the unstoppable wave of the future for the entire world — now faces an uncertain tomorrow even in the West. Pat Buchanan noted in a recent column, "Liberal democracy is in a bear market. Is it a systemic crisis, as well?" If it is, might authoritarianism and capitalism soon seem to be natural complements, the way that free markets and democracy were once thought to be?

111

Advocates of "democracy plus free markets" typically favor some variation of capitalism that is fused with popular elections, religious and cultural pluralism, secularized political institutions, tolerance of homosexuality, and women's rights. These seem to be the necessary preconditions for economic and moral well-being and for a peaceful international community, since, according to this particular picture of human history, democracies never fight each other.

At least to some extent, the identification of democracy with prosperity is true. The Fraser Institute's *Economic Freedom of the World, 1975-1995* and other more recent surveys show the correlation between high standards of living and "democratic institutions." Even such heavily taxed and regulated "democratic" countries as Sweden and Norway boast some of the world's highest living standards, as well as extensive domestic and foreign investments in their economies. Welfare states such as Australia, Iceland, Canada, and Sweden also register respectable rates of economic growth. That is because these countries, like our own, are politically stable and still have relatively unfettered economies.

But there is no reason to think that only governments that are "democratic" in the current usage can provide political stability and good investment climates. Free markets are operating well in very different political systems. One of the most successful examples of non-democratic capitalism is Singapore, which after winning independence in 1959 flourished under the firm hand of Lee Kuan Yew, who was prime minister or senior minister from 1959 until 2004. Lee has always stressed economic productivity and very low taxes. But in a 1994 interview with Fareed Zakaria, he pronounced his opposition to "Western democratic imperialism." While acknowledging that the U.S. has some "attractive features," such as "the free and open relations between people regardless of social status, ethnicity or religion" and "a certain openness in argument about what is good or bad for society," Lee expressed doubts about the American way "as a total system." "I find parts of it totally unacceptable," he told Zakaria, "guns, drugs, violent crime, vagrancy, unbecoming behavior in public — in sum the breakdown of civil society. The expansion of the right of the individual to behave or misbehave in public as he pleases has come at the expense of an orderly society."

In Lee's country — and in Asia more generally — they do things differently: "In the East the main object is to have a well-ordered society so that everyone can have a maximum enjoyment of his freedom. This freedom can only exist in an ordered state and not in a natural state of contention and anarchy." Lee had admired the U.S. in the past, but given the "erosion of the moral underpinnings" and the "diminution of personal responsibility" that has since taken place in recent decades, he has since changed his view of American democracy for the worse.

Contemporary Russia and China provide even more striking examples than diminutive Singapore of relatively free markets under authoritarian governments. But one need not look so far afield — the historical milieu in which capitalism arose in Europe supplies ample evidence closer to home. Industrial development in the West began long before European societies became "democratic" in the contemporary sense. Until the twentieth century, women didn't vote, nor did they hold extensive property rights. In many of the countries in which industrialization and the rise of the bourgeoisie first occurred, there was nothing like separation of church and state. And most of the Western societies that were undergoing industrial development in the mid- or late nineteenth century were not particularly tolerant toward labor unions: workers' strikes were often broken up by the police or the military. The Western societies that created free markets and expansive economies sometimes look almost medieval, as viewed from the perspective of contemporary "democracy." Yet these societies typically had freer — that is, less regulated — markets than our own modern states.

Conversely, present-day notions of democratic equality and what the state must do to promote that value may eventually preclude the possibility of relatively free markets. Despite their costly welfare states, Western democracies have so far been able to survive as wealth-producing countries, and this situation might have prevailed forever — if certain conditions of late democracy had not come along. In particular, feminist attitudes toward childbearing and the modern democratic state's affinity for mass immigration have clouded the future of free markets. To regard these culturally revolutionary features as merely accidental accompaniments of democratization is naive. They are inherent in the claims made by modern democracies to being pluralistic, egalitarian, and universalistic.

The current version of democracy benefits from consumer capitalism inasmuch as public administration needs the financial resources and consumer goods produced by the market to maintain social control. Consumer societies also serve the goal of democratic socialization — that is, the creation of "democratic," as opposed to "authoritarian," personalities — by encouraging a materialistic way of life. As Daniel Bell argues in *The Cultural Contradictions of Capitalism*, other things being equal, democratic-capitalist societies work against premodern institutions and values. A stress on consumption and on fashionable commodities leads to a condition of life characterized by the availability of ever-increasing goods and the association of social rank with their acquisition. Living in this manner nurtures both individual-centeredness and openness to change. These are values that democratic educators are happy to emphasize in order to weaken and replace traditional, pre-democratic communities.

But there are limits to how far democratic welfare states will go to sustain capitalism. Democracy's support of feminism, for example, creates short-term benefits but also long-term headaches for the economy. While today's working women earn and spend more than their predecessors who were not part of the labor force, they are also less focused than earlier generations on child-rearing, and are unable or unwilling to devote as much time and energy to their offspring. Among the results of women's emancipation from the family, particularly in Europe, has been a graying of the native population and the need to import a foreign, largely Third World, labor force. The rationale for this step has been to pay for retirement funds and social services, although more recently this policy has also been justified as helping to enrich the culture.

The gamble of importing unskilled immigrants to make up for the birth dearth has not paid off for Germany. Because of that country's bloated welfare state, its national debt is now eleven times higher than it was in 1972, and it is likely to increase fivefold in the next twenty years in order to provide social services to the new immigrants, the vast majority of whom are either unemployed or earning-impaired. Unemployment is now many times what it was in the 1970s. And the demographic collapse is only worsening. A prominent economist and onetime adviser to the Christian Democrats, Meinhard Miegel, in his monograph *Die Deformierte Gesellschaft,* draws a gloomy picture of a society that is falling on the skids materially, in a way that Freedom House and the Fraser Institute have avoided noticing. By 2200, if present trends continue, Germany will have the population that it did in 1800, but the demographic distribution will be the opposite: in 1800,

most Germans were below 40 years of age; already today 24 percent
are 60 or older. Although there are special circumstances in the German case, such
as the costs of national reunification, most of Germany's problems
are characteristic of other Western societies. Women marrying late
or choosing not to marry at all, low fecundity rates, and the welcoming of unskilled immigrants have all become endemic in the West.
Democracy today, with its emphasis on equality and pluralism, is an
agent of social disintegration.

It's also bad business. Although a modern democratic system can
coexist with capitalism in the short and even middle terms, the two
will eventually clash. Their contradictions are too glaring not to sur-
face. Expanding social programs, the lopsided statistical distribution
of young and old caused by the very democratic feminist movement,
and the importing of unskilled labor are bound to increase popular
demands for income redistribution. Our own country now stands at
the threshold of new social spending such as government-controlled
healthcare. While it might be hard to demonstrate that such developments have always inhered in a welfare-state democratic regime, one
can easily comprehend how modern democracy reached its present
state here and in Europe.

Can authoritarian governments conceivably do better than modern democracies as frameworks for capitalist economies? Certainly
the old idea that capitalist development inevitably leads to political
freedom has fewer adherents today than it did at the end of the Cold
War. Robert Kagan, in his new book *The Return of History and the
End of Dreams*, no longer treats the movement toward liberal democracy as "the unfolding of ineluctable processes," though he still calls
for the U.S. to form a "league of democracies" — an arrangement that
his admiring blurber, John McCain, intends to put himself in charge
of — to force the world to be free.

Once the reader looks beyond Kagan's search for enemies against
whom the "democracies" can mobilize their laggard populations,
however, one sees that he makes several relevant points. Authoritarian
powers like Russia and China can effectively integrate free market
economies into their nationalist projects. Economic freedom does
not necessarily require the adoption of liberal or democratic institutions. The belief that had driven the end-of-history theorists of the
1990s, that movement toward the free market would be accompanied

by political liberalization, has not proven consistently true, and the exceptions might be more important than the embodiments of the rule.

Although Kagan ignores the changing meaning of his god-terms "liberal" and "democratic," he correctly perceives the degree to which politics can control economics, even in a recognizable market economy. Not all capitalist economies will lead to the election of Barack Obama or Tony Blair. Indeed, in some societies a thriving economy may go hand in glove with a favored Russian Orthodox Church, the veneration of the last tsar and his family, or evocations of the glory of the Ming dynasty. To his credit, Kagan admits that capitalism does not always lead in the political direction he wants it to go. Market economies can be a valuable asset to any kind of government. Even those that prefer to rule by the stick have come to recognize the need for carrots.

Even so, autocratic capitalism may prove a transitory phenomenon, for the simple reason that authoritarian regimes are not likely to endure. Israeli political scientist Amos Perlmutter, the author of *Modern Authoritarianism*, argues that despotic governments rule in societies that are only imperfectly modernized: they have typically depended for their establishment on (often shifting) alliances made with the peasantry, military, established churches, and elements of the working class. Over time, such regimes either give way to other, similar orders — often as the result of military coups — or else they evolve, like Franco's Spain, Syngman Rhee's South Korea in the 1950s, and Pinochet's Chile in the 1980s, into middle-class constitutional states. Perlmutter does not have an ax to grind against authoritarian regimes, which often provide the breathing space for economic and political change. But he views them as stepping stones to periodic instability or else to democratic capitalism. Within this view, one does not have to agonize over a Singaporean exception, since Lee's attempt to blend economic growth with Confucian culture may not have any significance outside of his region. Lee may have produced an exotic flower that does not flourish in other climates.

It goes without saying that should authoritarian-capitalist states metamorphose into new democratic-capitalist regimes, they will soon be subject to all of the problems familiar to the West. And these difficulties will set in far faster than they did in our country because American cultural values will soon be swamping these fledgling democracies

— by example, if not by force. Given their longtime totalitarian pasts — and in China's case, far-flung, dense population — the modern malaise may take root in authoritarian lands more slowly than in more Westernized countries such as Japan. But the Chinese and Russian cases are not yet illustrations of a stable, long-term "authoritarian capitalism." Most likely, Putin and the Chinese Communists will eventually give way to "democratic capitalist" governments or to periodic regime changes followed, in the best of circumstances, by further economic growth. Without nurturing any illusions about the supposed friendship between democracy and capitalism, there is no compelling reason to treat autocratic capitalism as a permanent arrangement. The friendliest climate for economic freedom may have existed in pre-democratic Western societies in the nineteenth century. But that too proved to be a transition to something else, a new "democracy" with whose consequences we are still contending.

17. ILANA, ISRAEL AND THE PALEOS

Taki's Magazine, 16 January 2009

My friend Ilana Mercer has just posted a provocative essay on VDARE, which I would like to respond to. Ilana asks the timely question why the European Right has produced outspoken defenders of the Israeli government in its confrontation with Hamas, while in the U.S. by contrast the paleoconservatives have usually sided with the Palestinians. One should qualify this judgment, by pointing out that for several years until quite recently the Front National in France and the FPÖ in Austria leaned decidedly toward the Palestinians. Moreover, the support that Nick Griffin and his British National Party have given the Israelis is rather lukewarm and entirely predicated on the recognition that Muslims are a danger to Griffin's own nation. Griffin goes out of his way to stress the British interest that is at stake and to play down his concern with Israel or any other state in the Middle East.

In Germany, much of the anti-national Left is passionately pro-Israeli, on the goofy, anti-fascist grounds that by rallying to Israel, one could do more harm to a German national identity than by backing the Palestinians. (Germans, for those who may not have noticed, are obsessive masochists.) Meanwhile the nationalist Right in Germany, to the extent one still exists, has remained neutral in the current Middle Eastern conflict. Perhaps this Right, typified by the *Junge Freiheit* editorial board, is oscillating between being peeved over the anti-German statements coming from Jewish organizations and its predictable distaste for the Muslims now colonizing Europe.

There are also paleos who do not share the anti-Israeli stand that Ilana associates with the real American Right. I could mention my own case and could think of other paleos, beside Ilana, who back Israel, if one gave me enough time. But her general observation is correct. The European Right is generally more inclined toward the Israelis than are the American paleos, and the quotations taken from the Dutch

Freedom Party, the Vlaams Belang, and other European rightist parties that Ilana offers could be multiplied tenfold.

One possible reason for this transatlantic split is that the American Right is more sensitive than its European counterpart to the fact that Jews are typically on the left on social and political issues. In Europe Jewish organizations that support Israel have also typically backed Muslim immigration into Europe, and they have added insult to injury by jabbering about "Christian anti-Semitism" when the Muslim immigrants and their offspring start attacking Jews on the streets. In Australia Jewish organizations have been out in front demonstrating and signing petitions with Muslims to bar the anti-immigrationist, anti-Muslim Griffin from speaking down under. Jewish Zionists in the Diaspora have usually believed that while Christians are expected to back Israel to the hilt, Jews should be encouraged to work with Muslims and other non-Christians to secularize the culture and to bring multiculturalism to the host country. The Anti-Defamation League exemplifies these attitudes. To her credit, Ilana makes no attempt to justify this double standard.

But there are two other critical variables that distinguish our situation from the European. Unlike Western and Central Europeans, we have not had to face large-scale Muslim immigration, bringing in its wake anti-Christian Muslims and Islamic Fundamentalists. Although there has been an invasion from across our Southern border, that is a different can of worms. Unlike the Europeans and Israelis, we are not dealing with a large Muslim presence already inside our borders. Moreover, unlike Europeans we are not looking at entire sections of our country being occupied by Muslims. Such things are happening across the ocean, while multicultural governments are abetting this demographic trend and often punishing the indigenous Europeans who call attention to their situation.

Another variable concerns the primary enemies of the European and American Rights. In Western Europe there are neoconservative outposts, and as Richard showed in a recent spoof on Melanie Phillips, there are already English neoconservatives wishing to defend the West as an "abstract construct" or global democratic enterprise, by pledging undying support to the Israeli military. But such types are also less influential in Europe than they are in this country; and they are certainly not the main enemy that the populist, nationalist Right in Europe is confronting. In Europe the Right can take on the multicultural Left directly, without the problem of a second Left standing together with the rest of the Left against a more genuine Right. It has been the neoconservatives' success in marginalizing the Right that distinguishes our politics from that of Belgium or Switzerland. It also explains the virulent hostility toward Israel that now characterizes elements of the humiliated American Old Right.

Like Ilana, I regret this hostility; and like her, I think it is being targeted at a country that is fighting for its survival and whose geopolitical options have been exaggerated by its critics. Hamas is committed to the eradication of the "Zionist entity" and to expelling or killing its present Jewish population. Although wrongs were committed by all sides during the formation of the Israeli state, including the brutal persecution of Jewish populations in Arab countries as well as the uprooting of hundreds of thousands of Palestinians, we have to live in the present. The Israelis are trying to save their necks against implacable enemies, who from all indications have no desire to negotiate or strike bargains with them. This seems to be the case, despite the fact that the neoconservatives say exactly the same thing.

The question is whether I would reason this way about Israel absent certain factors: for example, if I had no Jewish blood, if members of my family had not fled Hitler and gone to Israel, and if my son-in-law were not an Israeli military officer. The answer is probably not. In this other reality I would be focusing during the present conflict on Israel's most boisterous advocates, including the neocons' underlings at *National Review* and *The Weekly Standard*. I would also be noticing all the others who run around sliming any critic of Israel as an anti-Semite or Holocaust-denier. Like Taki Theodoracopulos and Pat Buchanan, I would be sick of such defamers and their manipulation of the American Right. And such passions might affect my judgment about Israel.

While it may be grossly unfair that the Israelis should be caught in the crossfire, it is also inescapable. The man who is likely to become Israel's next premier, Benjamin Netanyahu, is a neoconservative mouthpiece. Netanyahu goes all over Creation making speeches about the need for global democracy and about how governments he and his neoconservative friends don't like are "undemocratic" and therefore "illegitimate." *The Jerusalem Post*, which is the largest English-speaking newspaper in Israel, is neoconservative from cover to cover. The same is true for the French edition that is now available on Israeli newsstands. Although most Israelis wouldn't know a neoconservative from a Dodo Bird, the image of their country that we have in the U.S. is filtered through neocon interpreters.

Why should American paleoconservatives see Israel's battle sympathetically? It would be nice if they did, but the fact that they don't is entirely understandable. As a point of information, the older generation of paleos was not always against Israel. Indeed one of the most outspoken critics of Israel, Pat Buchanan, spent years as a fervent advocate of the Israeli side. It was only when he noticed Zionist journalists dumping on the Catholic Church and trying to implicate it in the Holocaust that Pat moved in the opposite direction. One might ask why the Israelis should suffer for the idiocy of their cheering gallery? In an ideal world perhaps they would not, but in the world we inhabit countries do get held accountable for those who champion their cause.

Nor does it really matter that some of the advocates of the Palestinians are every bit as repugnant as those on the other side. These are not the people whom the paleos have been fighting for decades on a wide range of issues. Palestinian advocates may be tedious airheads but they don't impact the lives of paleoconservatives or paleolibertarians in any significant way. And when the advocates for the Palestinians show pictures of impoverished people huddled together in refugee camps, they are bound to elicit sympathy, no matter who fired the first missile where.

In conclusion, I would underline that I am not writing a refutation of Ilana's spirited polemic. The questions she provokes are important enough so as to warrant a detailed answer, which is what I have attempted to provide.

18. THE PATRON SAINT OF WHITE GUILT

Taki's Magazine, 19 January 2009

Today the American media, politicians of all stripes, and public educators will invariably fall into rapturous tones describing the black leader whose birthday is then being celebrated, namely, Martin Luther King (1929-1968). King's birthday is the only national holiday devoted to an individual American whose public observance has been commanded by Congress, and in 1983 this honor was accorded with more or less bipartisan support. The same tribute is no longer extended to the founder of our country George Washington, or to our sixteenth president, Abraham Lincoln, who is still widely honored for ending black slavery. Washington and Lincoln both now share a generic President's Day that is wedged in between their two birthdays in February. The gallant Southern leader Robert E. Lee, whose birthday coincides with King's and who after 1983 was to be co-celebrated in Southern states along with the black civil rights leader, has now fallen upon exceedingly hard times. Lee has become a non-person or even worse, someone identified with Southern slavery, although there is nothing to suggest that this Christian gentleman favored that institution or that he led the Confederate forces in Virginia for any reason other than the one he gave upon turning down an invitation to command the Union army — to protect his ancestral state against invasion.

There is a very clear relation to be drawn between these two recent developments, as my longtime friend Sam Francis delighted in pointing out. The replacement of Lee and Washington, who were related through Washington's wife Martha, by King as the center of a public cult signaled a true "iconic revolution" in our country. Nor was this revolution in consciousness likely to end with the congressional enshrinement of King or with the public acknowledgement of his birthday. Every January, there takes place an orgy of guilt-tripping and pseudo-Christian penance, one that seems to become shriller and more robotized with the passing of time. There is also in the U.S.

a relation between the downplaying of Christmas, which is being reduced here no less than in Britain to a "holiday season," and King's birthday in mid-January, which is followed by Black History Month, formerly known as February. What the new liturgical season highlights is King's martyrdom in 1968, when he was assassinated while leading a garbage employees' strike in Memphis, Tennessee, and the need for national atonement for our country's long embedded white racism. This penance, which is a post-Christian form of Lent, goes on through Black History Month and is then resumed for another putative victim group during Women's Month. Although the establishment Right (that is, GOP operatives and neoconservative journalists) and the Left disagree on how this sacral calendar is to be observed, they all see eye-to-eye on its contents.

The dispute here resembles nothing so much as the councils of the early Church that were devoted to clarifying the nature of Christ. Instead of the strife released over whether the concept of *homoousia* or that of *homoiousia* properly described the nexus between the first two members of the Trinity, we now have a more timely question: Did Martin Luther King, by his suffering and death, release our country from further atonement for racism or must this atonement become even more frenzied because of how his "unfinished mission for racial justice" ended?

Although the Heritage Foundation proclaimed King to be a "Christian theologian" as well as a "great conservative thinker," the reality is exactly the opposite: this now beatified figure was a self-proclaimed social radical, who provided the god figure of a post-Christian religion, albeit one that is parasitic on Christian narratives. He is living proof of the continuity between Christian images and a now victorious leftist ideology.

Lest I be accused of being unfair to my subject, let me stress that he was not really responsible for this glorification. As far as I know, King could never have imagined how he would be used after his death, any more than Karl Marx could have imagined that his ideas would be cited to justify Soviet tyranny. He might even have had the decency to blush if he had heard our "conservative" presidential candidate John McCain apologizing last spring in Memphis for having not supported the King public holiday soon enough. McCain characterized this failure as "the single biggest mistake in my political life."

Moreover, there is much about King's life that should command our respect, and particularly his personal courage. During his crusade against segregation in the Deep South and in his fight for black voting rights in the same region, he stood up against threats to his life. These went on from his participation in the boycott of segregated public transportation in Montgomery, Alabama, in 1955 down to his voting rights march in Selma in 1965. Throughout this period, and actually down to his violent death, King had to deal with hostile opponents, who threatened danger to him and his family. Not surprisingly, he was arrested and put in jail in Birmingham in 1963 for his violation of municipal ordinances. But King also made clear that while he was breaking laws that he found to be unjust, he was also willing to pay the penalty. And in his "Letter from a Birmingham Jail," penned in 1963, he shows as an ordained Protestant minister at least some acquaintance with theological sources that could be cited, however selectively, to legitimate his stand.

There is also much to object to about racial segregation. In its heyday it was extended to a plethora of public and private institutions, and, from what I recall, Jim Crow made few exceptions for worthy black would-be users of libraries and decent state universities. And Southern whites could have cleaned up this act for generations — before it became a *cause célèbre* for the Left and government social engineers. While no one comes in second to me in lamenting the effects of the Civil Rights revolution and especially its excesses, it would be foolish to deny that it began with a just cause. The same is of course equally true of other political disasters such as the French Revolution.

As someone whose family suffered grievously under the treaties ending World War One and later under the Nazi regime, it seems to me that complaints about the first were justified even if vicious people later exploited them. And there is no need to believe that by criticizing civil rights activists, one is expressing approval for what they sometimes correctly brought to public attention. Forcing some elderly black lady to sit in the back of a bus because of her skin color is not only degrading. It also provided a moral excuse to get federal bureaucrats and judges into the never-ending enterprise of reconstructing American society — an experiment that has now been extended to every aspect of our communal and commercial lives.

I would even surmise that had the issue of racial segregation not become a major national moral concern, with considerable media assistance, King and his organization, the Southern Christian Leadership Conference, would not have been able to move as easily as they did, with broad national endorsement, into mobilizing black voters. Our Voting Rights Act was passed in 1965, with disproportionate support from the Republican Party, to ensure federal supervision of areas in the South in which blacks had been kept or were suspected of having been kept from voting. Such steps contributed considerably toward moving our electorate toward the social Left, where about 99 percent of the black electorate can now be found. The leftward lunge in our presidential politics — represented by the recent victory of social leftist and, as Steve Sailer has revealed, black nationalist, Barack Obama — has been made possible by the changes accompanying the civil rights revolution, namely a large black electorate on the left that supports, with few exceptions, Obama and a white population that has been relentlessly instilled with a sense of racial guilt. Quite possibly, if the South had voluntarily desegregated its institutions, or had displayed more flexibility about race relations, some of this radicalization could have been avoided. By creating an eyesore, Southern whites contributed to the storm that later erupted.

It is not hard to show that King was a badly flawed public figure. But one can no longer do that in the U.S. without being suspected of being a "right-wing extremist" — often by self-described "conservatives" in the press. King's frequent acts of plagiarism, extending from his doctoral dissertation to his renowned "I Have a Dream" Speech delivered at the Washington Mall on August 28, 1963, have long been matters of record. One diligent scholar, Theodore Pappas, has devoted an entire work, *Plagiarism and the Cultural Wars*, to identifying King's borrowed sources. Pappas proves to what extent King as an orator and author engaged in "voice-dubbing" and "textual borrowing," as the mainstream media have referred to his frequent verbal thefts.

He was also a notorious philanderer who was not above using his pastoral activities to "counsel" young, voluptuous women. Some of his own advisors complained that his amorous activities got in the way of his political activities, although in his defense it might be argued that he had plenty of time for both. His connection to Communist friends, and most notoriously from 1957 onward to veteran Communist Party activist Stanley Levison, and the pop-Marxist phrases that laced his political commentary suggest that King was something other than the "Christian" idealist whom the GOP have discovered in his biography.

In his defense it is questionable whether King would have had anything but contempt for those "conservative" publicists who have tried to turn him into an advocate of free market economics, meritocracy, and war-mongering American patriotism. King already in the 1950s had called for government-introduced racial quotas in employment; he was also demonstrably a socialist with Marxist overtones in economics, and he famously denounced the Vietnam War as a struggle that hurt blacks by delaying their quest for equality. Although King had indeed just grievances, at least in the beginning of his career, his politics quickly descended into those of his disciple Jesse Jackson.

But my purpose is not to run him down. It is rather to stress his unsuitability for the role into which he was thrust after his death. I still recall standing in line to buy stamps in a post office in 1983 when a mother was explaining to her son who was looking at a newly minted stamp: "No, that's not the famous Martin Luther. It's a monk who was born five-hundred years ago, somewhere in Europe." This woman had, if anything, understated King's rising value, which was not to replace the father of the Protestant Reformation but Luther's savior. For this is certainly what King has become, a martyred deity, in today's American political culture.

19. VICTOR'S HISTORY

The American Conservative, March 2009

omeone ought to write a book called *Down the Memory Hole.* It would discuss the multifarious beliefs that American conservatives held until the second half of the twentieth century but subsequently gave up without fuss or embarrassment. Conservative leaders have not only abandoned their forebears' understanding of such events as the Civil War, World War I, and the civil rights movement, they have imposed on their followers exactly opposite views. A case in point is the revisionist historiography of Larry Schweikart, co-author — with Michael Allen — of *A Patriot's History of the United States.*

Schweikart, a regular on Fox News, takes to task "leftist" historians who disparage America's past or glorify the expansion of public administration. In the latter respect, he offers a useful antidote to the mainstream liberal history of my youth, particularly to exaggerated claims about FDR pulling us out of the Depression. Schweikart also tells the truth about such productive, non-activist presidents as Calvin Coolidge and Dwight Eisenhower, who have long been treated by left-leaning court historians as inferior to the leaders who built the welfare-warfare state. Schweikart notes the integrity of Grover Cleveland — one of our most morally upstanding but largely ignored chief executives — and dares bring up the discomfiting fact that most of those in the State Department whom Joe McCarthy deemed to be security risks were exactly that.

Yet many of the views that this patriotic historian considers far leftist are actually those of the Old Right. And notably, war and the social upheavals associated with it are the subjects where the revisionism is most glaring. Schweikart and other historians attached to the conservative movement define patriotism as defending wars that our government involved us in — or, beyond that, affirming that America is "the greatest country that ever existed."

Presumably, if America is now the most admirable country of all time, the devastations that got us where we are must all be celebrated. American pride has come to center on praising the present, which is supposedly under siege from the anti-American Left. The problem here is that the Left has even more reason than the patriotic Right to be proud of the American present. After all, culturally and politically, the Left has created American history as we now know it — a narrative of ever greater progress toward personal and group emancipation, which culminates in our offering the fruits of democracy to the world. To question the price of this achievement in war and bloodshed is to be unpatriotic as well as politically incorrect.

Conservatives' understanding of history changed profoundly between the 1950s and the 1980s — not because of superior evidence coming to light and forcing a reevaluation but because of new political agendas. As neoconservatives migrated from Left to Right, they brought with them what in the 1950s had been thought of as the Cold War liberal or "consensus" interpretation of history. Between the 1960s and 1980s, neoconservative and Old Right views of history clashed, particularly in the vituperative disputes over Lincoln's place in the American pantheon. Willmoore Kendall, Frank Meyer, and M. E. Bradford saw Lincoln as our own Caesar, and Kendall warned of "an endless series of Abraham Lincolns ... each prepared to insist that those who oppose this or that new application of the equality standard are denying the possibility of self-government, each ultimately willing to plunge America into Civil War rather than concede his point." By contrast, Harry Jaffa, a Lincoln enthusiast, declared that views like Kendall's amounted to "a distinctive American fascism, or national socialism."

The Jaffaites prevailed. Today, hardly anyone in my heavily Republican region of Pennsylvania can imagine criticisms of Abraham Lincoln, Woodrow Wilson, or FDR's prosecution of World War II as anything other than anti-American.

Among the perspectives that no longer belong to the establishment Right but that could once be found regularly in the *American Mercury, Human Events, National Review*, and other conservative publications are the following: Woodrow Wilson and his outspokenly Anglophile secretary of state, Robert Lansing, maneuvered us into World War I by treating the two belligerent sides unequally and excusing the British blockade of Germany, which was illegal under international law and starved German civilians. FDR behaved recklessly in dealing with imperial Japan in 1941, and whether he willed it or not, his actions were bound to lead to a Japanese attack. After Pearl Harbor, the U.S., led by such liberals as FDR and California governor Earl Warren, stripped American citizens of Japanese ancestry of their property and freedom as part of an attempt to frighten Americans into submission to the central government. (Significantly, Robert Taft was the sole Senate vote against internment.) The Nuremberg trials were an example of victor's justice that had no legal basis outside of the will of the anti-fascist winners, including Stalin. Moreover, World War II could have ended without insisting on "unconditional surrender" from the Axis powers; dropping atomic bombs on the Japanese was unnecessary for bringing about a just peace.

Nowadays, Richard M. Weaver's characterization of Allied behavior during World War II would surely get him branded as an "unpatriotic conservative":

"Our nation was treated to the spectacle of young boys fresh out of Kansas and Texas turning nonmilitary Dresden into a holocaust which is said to have taken tens of thousands of lives, pulverizing ancient shrines like Monte Cassino and Nuremberg, and bringing atomic annihilation to Hiroshima and Nagasaki. ... Such things are so inimical to the foundations on which civilization is built that they cast into doubt the very possibility of recovery."

Neoconservative historiography prevailed against the Old Right because it could build on the Left's moral assessments — treating Lincoln and General Sherman as great emancipators, for example — while at the same time tapping into the patriotic, pro-military sentiments of American Republicans and Fox News-viewing conservatives. From the liberal establishment's perspective, American history's new "patriotic" heroes — war presidents Lincoln, Wilson, FDR, and Truman — are a vast improvement over cantankerous Old Right figures like Robert LaFollette and Robert Taft.

Widespread historical illiteracy may also help explain the success of the new historiography. Selling young Republicans on myths, like Martin Luther King being a "conservative Christian," is remarkably easy. Indeed, it must be exhilarating to learn, as one of my Republican students announced in a senior seminar, that "all those people the Democrats like were really conservatives."

The neoconservative picture of our past was already so pervasive by the 1980s that even otherwise sound conservatives fell prey to it. From 1983 until 1988, Senator Jesse Helms, whom one could not plausibly accuse of being an FDR worshipper, opposed giving even nominal redress to Japanese-Americans who had been interned during World War II. Through most of this period, Helms enjoyed the support of the onetime New Dealer Ronald Reagan, who finally gave in and signed a bill sponsored by two Japanese-American Democratic congressmen. It is a sign of historical madness that liberals in the party of FDR were able to put themselves at the head of this movement to atone for leftist, anti-fascist sins, while the arch-conservative Helms attacked it endlessly as "unpatriotic." Had Helms known the truth, he would have sponsored his own bill and asked Norman Mineta and Robert Matsui to disavow FDR and his radical leftist destruction of civil liberties for Japanese-American citizens in good standing.

Ironically, the older Left and the Old Right occasionally agreed in their interpretations. The socialist literary critic Edmund Wilson in *Patriotic Gore* indignantly criticized the Union side in the Civil War for devastating the American South. And one of the most prominent critics of Woodrow Wilson was the Marxist historian William Appleman Williams, whom the anti-war Right still cites as an authority. As late as 1956, when Ted Sorenson ghostwrote *Profiles in Courage* for the soon-to-be Democratic presidential candidate John F. Kennedy, liberal Democrats could still extol figures and deeds that neoconservatives and neoliberals today would never tolerate. Sorenson included Robert A. Taft, for example, as a profile in courage for his opposition to the Nuremberg trials.

Today's academic and journalistic Left would never applaud such politically incorrect heroism — nor would movement conservatives. Except for American participation in the Cold War, the modern Left and the patriotic Right celebrate most of the same milestones on the American path to progress. Looking at Sean Wilentz's well-received *The Rise of American Democracy: From Jefferson to Lincoln*, it is difficult to find critical points over which the self-described liberal Democrat and Princeton luminary and his neoconservative readers might disagree. Although Wilentz and the patriotic school might wrangle over some aspects of FDR's New Deal policies, they would see eye to eye on most things, including the Civil War, Reconstruction, Wilson's presidency, U.S. conduct in the Second World War, and the civil-rights revolution.

This broad area of agreement about heroes and villains — and about how we reached the glorious present by overcoming the prejudices of the past — unites the liberal and patriotic versions of American history. This is the new consensus history, and it leaves little room for the Old Right's take on the past to get a fair hearing.

20. A Man in Full

The American Conservative, September 2009

My father was not the nicest person I have known. His temper was legendary, and despite his middling physical appearance and a bald pate that he had acquired in his thirties, he prided himself on his supposed good looks. He held grudges with extraordinary tenacity, and he never let us forget who had done him dirt.

One can, however, credit him with at least equally extraordinary qualities. He would have given his shirt away in a fit of generosity, and despite my mother's stern warnings, he was always lavishing money on relatives. He displayed extraordinary talent in the applied sciences: he not only built and wired additions to the house in which I grew up when he was in his late sixties; he also designed apparatus for the Bridgeport Fire Department. For many years he served on the municipal Fire Commission and as an *ex officio* member of the Police Commission.

In his fiery courage, my father had nothing in common with today's feminized and media-acceptable males. He had not distinguished himself as a soldier, but in his readiness to risk his life for a matter of honor, he did not much differ from the old exemplars of valor. Once, when he was already advanced in years and in visibly failing health, several local toughs, who had followed my parents back from a shopping mall, broke into their house and held them up at knifepoint. When they ordered my father to lie on the floor, he responded, "The hell I will." Picking up a lamp, he smashed it over the head of one of the three robbers. Another one delivered a glancing punch, which my father mostly avoided before striking his assailant back. Thereupon the robbers ran out of the house with my father in frenzied pursuit. It seems that these malefactors had been arrested for other break-ins, but those who had evidence of their crimes had been too frightened to press charges. My father made sure they were rearrested and told his assailants that if he saw them prowling around, he'd be delighted to kill them with the gun he stored upstairs.

Needless to say, he suffered in no way from the politics of guilt. He refused to work with the Fire Commission when he learned that it had established lower standards for black applicants. He also urged the fire captain to stay out of certain minority-occupied projects, in which the inhabitants had a tendency to pelt firefighters with stones and trash. Although a refugee from the Nazis who probably lost family members in the Holocaust — he could never determine how his half-brother and his children perished during the war — Dad would go ballistic if someone tried to misapply the "lessons" of Nazi genocide. He never blamed American Christians for what had been done by European Nazis, and he grew particularly exasperated if someone tried to draw dishonest implications from what had befallen Nazi victims. He did not think that the American civil rights revolution was "mandated" by events that unfolded in Hitler's Germany or Stalin's Russia, and he would go speechless with rage if someone suggested that Jews were morally required to support a porous border with Latin America because a ship of German Jews had not been allowed into the U.S. in 1940. In his view, such contrived parallels were utterly specious. They were made to fit a contemporary political agenda — one that he definitely did not support.

On one big issue we disagreed, but I never pushed my father to justify himself because I enjoyed the reasons for his predilection. He adored FDR and would take my brother and me to tour the Roosevelt estate at Hyde Park. There he would rhapsodize about the achievements of the president, who is buried behind his ancestral home, overlooking the Hudson, next to his Scottie Fala. Although "naïve about Stalin," FDR had kept Hitler from overrunning Europe and killing all of my father's relatives. Beyond his attainments in international affairs, FDR had done "some good things" at home, although the list of such accomplishments, even in Dad's telling, was limited. They consisted of closing the banks when he took office and his bold decision to take derelicts off the street and to send them to work camps. My father viewed FDR as the American counterpart of a European strongman, an authoritarian leader who avoided the excesses of Hitler and Stalin but who meant business when addressing staggering economic problems. An American libertarian would have struck him as at least as strange as a feminist.

Born in Budapest on December 24, 1911, my father felt comfortable in a world of fixed authorities, albeit one in which, as a boy, he had stood at the outer edge. His mother's family had been affluent, assimilated Austrian Jews. My grandmother came from Graz, the capital of Styria. But she had abandoned her first husband and my Uncle Emil for a tailor she met in Vienna. The two had gone off to the Hungarian capital, which was then a largely German-speaking city, one in which my grandparents failed to prosper. The irregular relationship between them — both had forsaken their earlier households — resulted in poverty and social exclusion for their three children, of whom my father Andrew was the youngest. His concern with structures of authority might have been affected by the fact that he grew up as an outcast of his mother's family and broader society. Most of his adult life was spent working his way into bourgeois respectability, first in Europe, and then, from the late 1930s on, in the United States.

His childhood was marred by memories of war, defeat, and popular turmoil. His first school became a hospital for wounded soldiers from the Austro-Hungarian army during the First World War. After his country had lost that struggle and suffered occupation, a Communist revolution broke out in 1919, resulting in the establishment of the ill-fated and inept Bela Kun regime. This disaster made way for a rightist regency under Admiral Miklós Horthy, which the Allies helped to install in a strife-ridden Hungary. Every change seemed in my father's young mind to bring increased problems, from human loss to Communist violence to a dishonest and intermittently anti-Semitic government, pretending to stand for the defeated Hungarians but really shilling for Hungary's enemies. Despite these circumstances, my father prospered as a master furrier. His family had had him apprenticed in this once lucrative trade, and he was able to rise through the ranks. By the time he had reached his mid-twenties and had become the owner of a store in a plush sector of Pest, he was leading the life of a *bon vivant*.

He decided to come to the United States for two reasons. After the assassination of Austrian Chancellor Engelbert Dollfuss in July 1934 at the hands of Nazi agents, he assumed that it was only a matter of time before Hitler "liberated" the Alpine Republic and integrated Austria into the German Reich. Paramilitary groups that imitated the German Nazis were already operating in Hungary, a problem that the authoritarian regime of Horthy became increasingly powerless to handle.

There was also a large underground Communist Party, which was subservient to Moscow and looked back on the expropriations and summary executions of the Kun interlude with undisguised nostalgia. My father surmised that Hungary would soon be the plaything of rival tyrannies. It was best to get out while he had time.

The second reason was that my father's sister Regina was married to a Hungarian Jewish sharecropper who apparently had struck it rich in the New World. As luck would have it, he had been born in the U.S. while his parents were briefly sojourning there at the beginning of the twentieth century. Somehow this American-born brother-in-law had managed to bring my grandmother to New York, a fate she bitterly lamented. She had been uprooted twice, she complained, and having left Austria for Hungary, where the people spoke some weird Turkic language, she now found herself among the "*ungezogene Kinder* [badly behaved children]" of Anglophone America.

Unlike his mother, my father adjusted quickly. He mastered English except for his tendency to substitute German possessive pronouns. He also obtained employment, again as a furrier, repairing coats for large dealers. But he had to change jobs periodically because of his lack of a "red book." Apparently only Communist Party members were supposed to work in these shops. My father, who found the Communists vulgar, refused to join their movement. At one point, he had to hide on a fire escape when the Communist organizer came to check on the party membership of employees. Dad was warned that party thugs had a way of punishing non-members who presumed to work in a "party shop." He left to work for a large fur business in Bridgeport, Connecticut, and once he had collected enough capital, opened his own shop.

This loner who read Hungarian literature and did complicated home repairs during his leisure hours somehow found time to meet and marry my mother. My maternal grandfather, the uncle of Regina's husband, showed himself to be extremely hospitable to my father. Papa (my grandfather) was hard-working and frugal to a fault: he would walk from his apartment to the fur dye factory he owned in Greenpoint, near the Brooklyn Naval Yards, rather than spend a few cents on a streetcar. He believed that the pennies added up — especially if one had to work at least six days a week. My grandmother would wake no later than 3:00 a.m. to prepare her husband's breakfast and lunch, and Papa would be off to work before sunrise. During the day, he would do the heavy lifting in his factory because he didn't want to deal with unionized workers. Better, he thought, to drag around heavy barrels of chemicals at age 75, with fingernails disfigured by dyes, than rely on whiny union men.

Papa took instantly to my father, who came to visit a few weeks after he had arrived in New York and bedazzled his distant relative through marriage with Old World *savoir-faire*. My mother likewise fell for this visitor, although he was "much older," by seven and a half years, and was imagined to have led a perhaps "questionable" social life in Europe. The couple was married about five years later, after what was considered a proper courtship.

The home my parents set up would include some of my father's immigrant relatives and, most disturbingly, my paternal grandmother, who ruled like a Chinese matriarch. I respect my mother deeply for having put up with this forbidding lady and above all with the unpleasantness of having to listen to her rail against American social immorality. Although herself no paradigm of bourgeois virtues, she condemned those in whose country she had taken refuge for being self-indulgent.

My father became a constant companion to his father-in-law, who survived two wives and eventually came to live with us. I have never known a more dutiful son-in-law than my father was in looking after my ailing and eventually senile grandfather. It was as if he felt a deep debt of gratitude to this man who had given him his daughter when he was but a newly arrived immigrant.

My father always included Papa when he took my brother and me on Sunday outings in his early-1950s Pontiac. These trips involved visiting some nearby Connecticut town or chugging along Route 7, which hugged the New York state line. On special occasions, we would travel as far as Boston or Philadelphia, but would always come back the same day. And we would usually bring along a basket full of sandwiches, consisting of roast beef or turkey from Friday evening's meal. My father's first major trip after many decades in the U.S. was back to his native city in the mid-1960s. He was not especially impressed. Budapest under Communist rule, he told us, looked much shabbier than Paris, Vienna, Jerusalem, or any of the other foreign cities he thereafter visited.

It may behoove me to protect my father from a charge leveled against him by my mother. Dad was considered to be a spendthrift who would have left his family with little had he died in his forties or fifties. Here a distinction may be in order between the generosity that Aristotle thought worthy of a free man (*eleutheroprepes*) and the habits of a wastrel. My father's giving fell into the first category, one that the philosopher famously praised as an aristocratic trait in the *Nicomachean Ethics*. Dad hastened to help out the family of his older brother when my uncle fell ill with terminal lung cancer. He would also receive houseguests with effusive hospitality, and when I was a graduate student at Yale, he would invite home my classmates and their spouses for dinner. My father was particularly kind to one of my older classmates, who could never muster the energy to finish his dissertation on the Assyrian concept of time. Laszlo came from a distinguished Hungarian family that had held high positions in the Horthy government. Unfortunately, this offspring of gentry was a nervous, diminutive man who chain-smoked and could never put his life in order. Each time he tried to describe his puzzling dissertation topic, Laszlo would plunge into a state of nervous exhaustion.

Looking at my parents, I devised the theory of "aesthetic equivalence." Most couples are roughly equivalent in terms of physical attractiveness. Young people develop an intuitive sense of their relative marketability in appealing to the opposite sex. When one encounters a highly attractive man or woman married to a less physically appealing mate, one looks for special factors that might have affected this unusual selection.

In my parents' case, there was a degree of aesthetic disparity that I noticed even as a pre-adolescent. My mother, quite simply, was much better looking than my father. She had a delicate bone structure and a sweet, girlish face. But Dad had presence and loads of Old World charm, an intoxicant that my Greek friend Taki Theodoracopulos exudes. My late wife Dana commented on this magnetic quality when she first met my father in 1968. She found him initially far more pleasing than my mother because of his attentiveness to women, particularly those whom he was encountering for the first time. He was also a splendid ballroom dancer, unlike his two sons, who have drawn whispers on the dance floor by being flat-footed embarrassments.

It was this sense of command, what the Romans called *auctoritas*, that stood out among his positive qualities. Bridgeport had a large Hungarian-speaking community, and one of the reasons that my father and his family had settled there was the possibility of conducting business in Hungarian while working to pick up English. Dad developed extensive social and commercial contacts there, and although he only attended religious services on special occasions, he joined the synagogue on the west side of our then bustling industrial hub, in what was called "Hunkeytown." The congregation had been founded in 1909 by "young men from Hungary," as the charter explained. The founders had almost all gone back to Europe afterwards and had fought in the Austro-Hungarian army during World War I. Many returned to Bridgeport years later, after odysseys in South America and Europe.

Within this community, my father was accorded respect as a man of standing, and people would come to our house seeking his advice about personal and business matters alike. Although largely self-educated, he seemed by the standards of a transplanted peasant culture to be someone who truly stood apart. Years later, when my brother drew a distinction between our immigrant father and my brother's wife's parents, who had attended prestigious American universities generations ago, I could not grasp how our father had occupied a lower social level. He seemed in my view to have done better than I had. His name is on the cornerstones of the firehouses in Bridgeport. In the Hungarian community he was always respectfully addressed as *Gottfried Úr*, a term that suggested something more exalted than "Mister."

My father's *auctoritas* was on display when the mayor asked him for a particular favor. His district was about to hold an election for alderman, and since the Republican Party would likely pick up the seat on the city council, it was imperative to find a candidate who would vote with the Republican mayor. Nick asked Dad to come up with someone whom he thought might fit the bill. My father settled on a young, recently married fellow whose parents he had known well and told him to come by the house to speak to him. When Burton arrived and my father asked if he would like to be alderman, his young guest began to get chummy, calling his host "Andy" then launching into a speech about how he would "improve this place." My father scowled and proceeded to lay down the law. He was Commissioner Gottfried, and if Burton wanted the nod, he would have to promise not "to yap about naïve programs" but to vote with Mayor Panuzio.

This *auctoritas* became less impressive as my father aged. In his mid-sixties he fell into an unseemly quarrel with my wife Dana's father while both were visiting us. Dana and I understood what was taking place: our fathers had been hard, resourceful men whose self-worth was growing brittle as they became older. They had also drunk more Scotch than they should have. While working to set up a swing set for our youngsters in the backyard, they began to raise their voices. By late afternoon, they were insulting one another, and only by separating them did we avoid a further escalation of hostilities. By evening, the storm had passed, but I don't remember seeing Dad and my father-in-law show much in the way of friendship toward each other again. By then both were exhibiting the effects of too much drinking and of noticeable arterial deterioration. What had angered Dana's father, a dignified physician with vast humanistic learning, were my father's boastful expressions of self-importance. Ten years earlier, I could not have imagined him acting in this manner. As a younger man, he had taken his talents in stride and would have been irritated by the behavior for which my father-in-law berated him.

By the time he died in 1987 it was only by virtue of my age that I could remember him as someone who had once been an authority figure who soared above his companions. I recall my sense of disbelief when he visited me for the last time, after we had moved to a Washington suburb. By then Dad was doddering and quite deaf, and it was hard for me to associate him with the titan I had once relied on. Then the unexpected happened. Our basement began to fill up with water when one of the spring downpours wrought havoc on our property. My father ran down to the basement and found a sump pump, which he got to work. Before long he had my five children and me lugging pails of muddy water up to the front door. Within an hour, my father had the problem under control.

The water would return the following week, when the next downpour occurred. But the beautiful part of the incident was that it allowed my family and me to see my father one last time as he had once been — obviously in command. Even in his final months, as his energy ebbed, his old and truest self shone through.

21. The Myth of "Judeo-Christian Values"

Alternative Right, 12 April 2010

Reading Larry Auster's website over the years, I find there is much in his spirited commentaries that I agree with. Larry's attacks on liberals and neoconservatives, his stress on the enormous overlap between these two only minimally different groups, his focus on the immigration issue, and his critical examination of the government's war on traditional social relations and religious morals are invariably of high quality. Larry dares to say things that one would rarely see in mainstream liberal and neoconservative publications, and therefore we on the real right owe him a debt of gratitude for these efforts.

An issue, however, that he and I strongly disagree about is his conception of a Judeo-Christian war against Islam. First, I have never shared Larry's fierce revulsion for all Muslims as bearers of violence and hatred. I have known practicing Muslims for most of my life, and among them I have numbered personal friends. I have also never perceived any signs of violence or malice in dealing with these Muslims. Last Sunday my wife and I were with a young Turkish couple in a Turkish restaurant in Allentown, Pennsylvania; and I found nothing off-putting about the Muslims I saw coming in to eat *Halal* food. They looked, acted, and ate like the Orthodox Jews whom I have known, and I felt much safer in their company than I would have felt among the inner-city minorities, who may be Pentecostal Christians. Such non-Muslims, in any case, were doing drug deals outside the restaurant in which we were dining.

Although I agree with Larry about the need for a moratorium on immigration, particularly from Latin America, and although I share his view that decadent, childless Europeans are committing physical and demographic suicide by repopulating their countries with lower-class Muslims, who often incline toward Islamic Fundamentalism, I strongly dissent from his unqualified generalizations about adherents of Islam.

Moreover, I think that there is something other than a sense of emergency that has fueled Larry's call for a Judeo-Christian front against Muslims as a collective enemy. To be very blunt (and I may be in view of the fact that Larry has scolded me more than once as a self-hating Jew), my friend may be addressing a personal problem when he grasps for conceptual straws, as a Jew who converted to Christianity. In order to bridge the poles in his hyphenated existence, he appeals to a desirable but, alas, fictitious unity. To say that Christians and Jews are both being targeted by Islamic Fundamentalists does not mean that they share a close friendship based on common religious convictions.

Larry may wish that such a community of belief in fact existed. And so do the Christian Zionists and the Christian employees of the neoconservatives, who share Larry's rhetorical habit when they refer to "Judeo-Christians." Admittedly one could describe Jesus, Peter, and Paul as Judeo-Christians but they may have been the last Jews who would answer to that description. In the first century total war broke out between two rival Jewish sects, the Pharisees and the Jewish Christians. While the Jews had the upper hand, which they didn't for very long, they went after the Christians, and from the High Middle Ages on, the Church paid back the Jews in a more devastating way, from a greater position of strength.

Significantly, the issues Jews had and still have with Christians are theological and cultural, as well as the result of persecutions inflicted on Jews by some European societies in the past. The central Christian beliefs, that God became man in Christ and atoned on the cross for human sins, are utter blasphemy from a Jewish or Muslim perspective. And the Rabbinic attacks on Jesus that are found in the Talmud are directed against the founder of Christianity as a blasphemer. David Gordon revisits all these facts in detail in a review of George Weigel's *Faith, Reason, and the War against Jihadism*. But let me add other facts. The Rabbinic attacks against Christian beliefs were not a response to Christian persecution since they were produced in Babylonia, in what was then a predominantly Zoroastrian society. The only Christians whom the authors of the Talmud were likely to have encountered were Monophysites, who rejected the Trinitarian statement formulated at Chalcedon and who were living in Babylonia as a powerless minority.

Second, Muslims have never represented for Jews the religious problem posed by Christianity because the theological and ritual differences between Jews and Muslims are far less significant. As Maimonides pointed out in the thirteenth century, Jews may pray to Allah because the Muslim and Jewish conceptions of the Deity are the same. The Muslim dietary and ritual laws and the strict separation of the sexes also resemble their Jewish equivalent, although Muslims are less strict than Orthodox Jews in dietary matters. Unlike Orthodox Jews, observant Muslims will eat meat slaughtered by a Jewish ritual slaughterer, but Orthodox Jews will not return the favor by eating *Halal* meat. While some Jews fled from the Catholic Inquisition by going to Calvinist Holland and Dutch New Amsterdam, far more Jews left for the Ottoman Empire, where they were allowed to live for centuries in peace.

Until the eruption of hostilities between Jews and Muslims over Israel, Jews in the West continued to speak far more favorably about Muslims than they did about Christians. I myself noticed this difference in my youthful contacts with Jewish institutions, which always treated the Muslim world in a far kinder way than the Christian West. My students, who have read the historical writings of Bernard Lewis, noticed the same characteristic in this Jewish author. Whenever he compares the two universal religions, Christianity and Islam, Lewis favors the Muslims at the expense of the Christians. A distinguished Jewish historian already in his seventies, he reflects traditional Jewish attitudes toward the core religious beliefs of the two religions in question.

Until the mid-1980s when the neoconservatives started building an alliance with the Christian Zionists, *Commentary* featured scathing invectives against the Christian belief system as well as the "crucifixion myth" as the source of the Holocaust. Larry might wish that Jews thought differently about Christian believers since he himself is one, but alas most of them don't. Jewish organizations here and in Europe view Christians as people whose exaggerated guilt over the Holocaust can be channeled into support for the Israeli government. Prominent Jewish groups, such as the World Jewish Congress, the Canadian Jewish Congress, and the Anti-Defamation League, show nothing but indifference or hostility to the continued existence of Christian institutions in what used to be Christian countries.

Such behavior is not restricted to countries in which established Christian churches once persecuted Jews. It is equally present in predominantly Protestant countries, which have no significant histories of anti-Semitism. Why do most American Jews loathe the philo-Semitic Christian Right, a religious force that only a lunatic would mistake for the anti-Jewish Russian Orthodox Church of the nineteenth century? In surveys about religious intolerance in America, as Norman Podhoretz rightly notes, Jews seem inordinately upset about Evangelical Christians, a group whose ethical positions are the same as those taught by Hebrew Scripture and who adore Israel almost as much as Larry.

My explanation, which Larry may not want to hear, is that Jewish distaste for Christianity is so deep-seated that it cannot be written off as a legacy of Christian anti-Semitism. This unfortunate hostility actually seems to grow in intensity or expressiveness as Christians try to reach out to Jews. Christophobia may be weakest among Jews in Muslim countries, who have only minimal dealings with Christians, or among Israelis, who view Christians as a distant ally. But these Jews would not be likely to go about celebrating Larry's "Judeo-Christian" values, although they might use, and have used, Christian Zionists as a link to Republican administrations, when the occasion presents itself.

I must also dissent from Larry's tendency to blame Jewish thinking about Christians on the effects of liberalism. Jews helped create and propagate this particular ideology largely as a protective device against an older Christian civilization. There might well be problems with the liberal ideas that Jews have supported until now, but it is simply wrong to pretend that Jewish liberals act from liberal motives that have nothing to do with their Jewish fears and hostilities. I've never met a Jewish liberal whose leftist politics was not in some way connected to his self-identity as a Jew. Larry might believe (and I wouldn't dispute his judgment) that this typically Jewish ideological stance is inappropriate for Bible believers or incompatible with long-range Zionist interests. But it is the way that Jews have responded to their anxieties in the Christian West. And mixed with this anxiety at some level is a sense of marginality grounded in theological difference. Here we come back to Larry's existential problem, which is his need to avoid confronting the Judeo-Muslim rejection of core Christian teachings.

These remarks are not intended to minimize the gravity of certain differences. Needless to say, I'd be delighted if Jews thought differently about the Christian world, which might end their tiresome attach-ment to what has become the cultural Marxist Left. But expressing this pious wish may be like wishing that elephants could fly. What seems unlikely, however, is that one could bring about an alternative reality by demonizing all Muslims. Indeed it is no longer even possible to be a crusading anti-Muslim without having to consort with Christopher Hitchens-secularists, feminists, and pro-gay rights liberals. Larry's holy crusade is certainly not going forth as a Christian, or "Judeo-Christian," enterprise. It has turned into a tacit alliance with the very people he professes to despise.

22. DON'T BLAME FASCISM

The American Conservative, July 2010

Behind Glenn Beck loomed the faces of Barack Obama, Hillary Clinton, the German philosopher Martin Heidegger and the American progressive John Dewey. The host gestured to the photos as he revealed the common link to Fox viewers: all favored state intervention in the economy and apparently did not believe in the concept of natural rights as found in the Declaration of Independence. Thus all of them flirted with fascism.

To drive home this point, Beck had invited Jonah Goldberg, author of *Liberal Fascism*, onto his program. Goldberg sees ominous connections between the economic corporatist Mussolini and the shenanigans of the current Democratic administration. To him, Hillary Clinton's notion that it takes a village to raise a child resembles nothing so much as the policies of Hitler's head of the German Labor Front, Robert Ley. This allegedly Nazi-esque rhetoric comes to Hillary by way of her longtime advisor Michael Lerner, a Jewish leftist. Like the Nazis, Lerner and presumably Hillary believe that "morality, politics, economics and ethics: none of these things can be separated from anything else." Indeed, the welfare state policies advocated by Lerner, according to Goldberg, look as if they were lifted from the Nazi platform of 1920.

Nor is that all: the vegetarian and ecological concerns of many Democrats seem similar to the beliefs of interwar fascists and Nazis. Hitler and Himmler prefigured these contemporary American fashions, Goldberg warns, as he notes that "many on the left talk about destroying whiteness in a way that is reminiscent of the National Socialist effort to de-Judaize German society." To anyone else the difference between these situations might seem obvious: while Hitler's plan was directed at a generally helpless minority in his country, the anti-white posturing of American journalists and educators is an acquired taste among the predominantly white elite.

145

But Beck and his guest are hardly the only movement conservatives who perceive a world fascist threat. Rudy Giuliani remains at war with "Islamofascism." Other Fox News luminaries, such as Charles Krauthammer, Sean Hannity, and Fred Barnes, are preoccupied with the same demon. Norman Podhoretz's *World War IV* is not surprisingly subtitled *The Long Struggle against Islamofascism*. Given these weighty authorities, it seems that fascism is America's number one enemy.

Fascists, real or imagined, have long been the European Left's preferred opponents. The f-word in Europe is directed against all who stand in the way of further gay and feminist rights or unlimited Third World immigration. Anyone on the wrong side of these issues is labeled a fascist, which really means Hitler. The Left is perennially fighting Nazis in the form of any position or figure deemed insufficiently progressive. And now American neoconservatives are getting in on the fun, but with a twist: just as European leftists are convinced that anyone concerned about historic nations and traditional morality is a fascist, so neocons are equally sure that fascism is fundamentally a left-wing phenomenon.

They are all wrong. While conservatives are not fascists, as the Left would have it, neither are fascists leftists, as Goldberg and company believe.

There were in fact different fascisms in the 1920s and 1930s, and they were not always on the same side. As late as 1934, the Italian fascist leader Mussolini tried to come to the aid of the Austrian clerical fascist Engelbert Dollfuss, whom Hitler's henchmen in Vienna finally assassinated. Not all fascists were racists or especially anti-Semitic, and until the Axis agreement was reached in 1936, it did not seem that Hitler and Mussolini would be on the same side in any future war.

Mussolini, who in 1922 became the first fascist to take over a European government, claimed to represent and embody a "national revolution," not a single class — such as the Italian proletariat — let alone the "workers of the world." Although *Il Duce* had once been an avowed man of the Left, the authoritarian government he constructed within what looked like a vestigial constitutional monarchy was not notably socialist once installed, although it claimed that all things were being done in the name of the state. Mussolini, as Goldberg correctly observes, had many admirers throughout the political spectrum, including the Black Nationalist Marcus Garvey, the Revisionist

Zionist Zeev Jabotinsky, and at least half the editorial board of *The New Republic*, which viewed him as a progressive state planner. Not until Mussolini's entirely unexpected alliance with the Nazis did world opinion turn against him — including the judgment of his erstwhile fans Franklin Roosevelt and Winston Churchill.

Garden-variety fascisms — in contrast to the partly Stalinized German Nazi form — were counterrevolutionary in character. The German historian Ernst Nolte describes the fascists as a "counterrevolutionary imitation of the Left." Fascist movements mobilized masses and made deals with the working class, but what allowed them to come to power was their armed opposition to the revolutionary Left. They flourished in countries with large anarchist and Communist movements. And while they promised national revolutions that would rise above selfish bourgeois interests and parliamentary squabbles, fascism relied, particularly in Italy, France, and Spain, on the support of a frightened bourgeoisie.

The fascists became the party of order. In Austria, the Jewish classical liberal Ludwig von Mises declared for the Catholic corporatist Right against the socialist revolutionary Left, which the clerical fascists were then keeping at bay. In the 1930s, European Communists targeted fascism as an especially insidious enemy. What they meant was not first of all Hitlerism but movements like Mussolini's. Even then the Communists and their allies correctly viewed the fascists as sham revolutionaries, who introduced only minor welfare measures once they came to power. In contrast to the dreams of the Left, the fascist revolution stressed hierarchy and the glorification of one's nation and its antecedents. While the Left took from the French Revolution a model for sweeping social reform, the Italian fascists admired the Revolution's appeal to classical antiquity and military heroism.

So why do so many movement conservatives today call everyone they dislike "fascists"? There are four reasons.

First, this rhetorical weapon allows self-styled conservatives to have some fun by applying to the other side a pejorative term that the Left has had a monopoly on. Such a tactic may be emotionally satisfying, but it is intellectually bankrupt. Only a cultural illiterate could believe that interwar fascists were intent on pursuing a massive welfare state centered on the achievement of social equality, with special protection for racial minorities, feminists, alternative lifestyles, and whatever else the latter-day Left is about. Republicans and Democrats share more of this agenda with each other than either does with interwar fascists.

America's major parties support a far more economically intrusive government than any that Dollfuss, Mussolini, or other non-Nazi right-wing corporatists tried to put into operation between the world wars. Until the outbreak of World War II, the Italian fascist government took a smaller percentage of income from families than American households are now required to fork over to our regime. Equally important, the Italian fascist state never attempted to manage gender relations and conversations about ethnicity. Unlike the politically correct postmodern state, it left social relations pretty much the same as they had been before.

The second reason for the American Right's anti-fascist rhetoric is historical. Some critics of FDR and the New Deal, such as Garet Garrett, Isabel Paterson, and John T. Flynn, believed that the American welfare state was the equivalent of the Italian fascist and later German Nazi regimes. But there is no reason to yield to their flawed judgments. These writers made the unwarranted leap from thinking that all forms of economic planning were unacceptable to believing that all were virtually identical. It is true that FDR, his Brain Trusters, and much of the American Left found a great deal to admire in Mussolini's experiments. But so too did conservative Catholics, who often professed admiration for European fascists' cultivation of good relations with the Church and the middle way they sought to forge between plutocracy and socialism. Not incidentally, U.S. anti-fascist critics of the New Deal tended to be American-style libertarians. They had a very limited understanding of the European Right or the European Left and usually threw "statists" of all kinds into the same rogues' gallery.

Much of today's talk about fascism derives from a third motive — a thinly disguised *reductio ad Hitlerum*. Whenever Krauthammer or Giuliani bring up "Islamofascism," we are being reminded that the enemies of Israel are like the Nazis. These enemies, it is implied, seek to inflict on the Israelis and the entire Jewish people what the earlier "fascist" Hitler almost succeeded in doing. The word "fascist" is meant to summon everyone to action against an implacable, existential military threat to the Israelis.

But the final and most fundamental reason for the establishment Right's anti-fascist pretensions is a deeply rooted leftist mindset in which fascism remains the world's greatest evil. In the 1980s, neoconservatives came to control the American conservative movement in what was mostly a friendly takeover. Conservative foundations and journals began sliding toward the Left, and in the new pantheon of conservative heroes one found such previously unlikely figures as Harry Truman, Woodrow Wilson, Abraham Lincoln, and eventually Martin Luther King.

The reconstructed Right continued to be anti-Soviet and generally anti-Communist. But while the post-World War II Right typically denounced the Communists as godless materialists striving for absolute equality, neoconservatives became anti-Communist for different reasons. They stood in the tradition of such Cold War liberals and pro-labor Democrats as Senator Scoop Jackson and AFL-CIO leader George Meany. The anti-Communist Left condemned the Soviets as oppressors of the proletariat and counterrevolutionaries posing as socialists.

In the neoconservative version of anti-Communism, the enemy remained on the Right. The Soviet dictatorship became what Truman described after World War II as "Red Fascism." This was also the way the German socialist Kurt Schumacher defined the new enemy after 1945, when he denounced the "red-lacquered Nazis." Unlike the old anti-Communist diatribes in *National Review*, *Human Events*, and *Modern Age*, later neoconservative anti-Communism, as Sam Francis once observed, gives evidence of a "leftist *gestalt*." The present "conservative" struggle shows the same *gestalt*, as it battles the recycled menace of interwar fascism.

Anti-fascist neocons are in fact far to the left of characters like Mussolini. The ghosts haunting American politics are not the specters of Heidegger or Hitler lurking behind Obama and Mrs. Clinton. They are the spirits of old anti-Stalinists like Trotsky that now possess the establishment Right.

23. THE INSPIRATION OF JOE SOBRAN

Alternative Right, 3 October 2010

The death of Joe Sobran on September 30, after several years of failing health, could not have come as a total surprise to any of his friends. News about his deteriorating condition and the need for divine intervention was steadily provided by Fran Griffin, his alter ego of many years, his longtime publisher, and, not least of all, his tireless fundraiser. From Fran's reports throughout September, it was clear that Joe would not survive much longer. The news that he expired painlessly may have been the least disturbing communication from her during this period.

Joe's death deprives those of us on the independent right and in Anglophone society of a brilliant literary presence. Although widely known as a political controversialist, Joe was also, not incidentally, one of the most impressive English stylists of his and my generation. Most of his columns, like his works on Shakespeare's real identity and on complicated constitutional questions, were literary gems. And though he would not have presumed to compare his talent to that of his hero G. K. Chesterton, Joe was probably Chesterton's equal as a master of expository prose. The reason this graduate of Eastern Michigan (and scion of a working-class Ukrainian family) rose rapidly at *National Review* to become a senior editor within three years, after being hired in 1972, is that William F. Buckley recognized his considerable talent.

And arguably Joe was kept at the magazine even after Norman Podhoretz and his soulmates condemned him as an anti-Semite in 1993, because Buckley wished to hold on to his best writer. Perhaps trying to bring around his newly acquired neoconservative dinner companions, Buckley defended Joe (and Pat Buchanan) for a time as "contextual" rather than genuine anti-Semites. According to Buckley, it was because of general sensitivity to the historic problem of anti-Semitism and the special place of Israel among American Christians as well as American Jews that the frontal attack on AIPAC and Jewish media power engaged in by Joe aroused such resoundingly negative feelings.

Joe retorted that if his targets were as weak and vulnerable as they claimed, then he would not have had to fear for his job and his future.

In the end he was driven off the pages of *National Review*, after violating a rule established for him specifically, that he would never again be allowed to write on Jewish subjects. I doubt Joe broke that rule out of disrespect for Buckley, whom he viewed as a second father. Meeting both of them at a conference at Hillsdale in the mid-1970s, I was struck by Joe's deferential behavior toward his mentor. Even after he lost his post at *National Review* and Buckley had become for the entire world to see the servile instrument of neoconservative power, Joe went on speaking of him with profound respect. In 2008, after Buckley had died, Joe, who by then was badly ailing, expressed relief that he had been able "to patch things up" with the man whom he had esteemed for so many decades.

If he had violated Buckley's house rule by returning to forbidden subjects, he had done so because he would not allow himself to be intimidated. And though I often disagreed with Joe's positions, or found them to be overstated, there were two things I would never question. One, the author in question was a person of unimpeachable integrity; and two; he would never have expressed an opinion simply in order to advance his career. By contrast, his enemies had no such virtues, and it was not surprising that Joe's adversary had made a reputation for himself by writing memoirs appropriately titled *Making It*. Joe's enemies stood for the Kingdom of Arrogance, although given how well they have done, one would have to reconsider the truth of the biblical teaching that "pride goes before the fall." This certainly has not been the case for those who ruined Joe's career.

It now seems to me that Joe's enemies won, at most, a Pyrrhic victory. They had derailed the careers of others, including Sam Francis and myself. They had also smeared Buchanan in their publications and then pummeled him with nasty accusations of anti-Semitism and homophobia during his presidential run in 1992. But Buchanan landed on his feet, and so did I, to the extent that I could fall back on some kind of academic position. Sam, too, survived after a fashion, even after the neoconservatives, led by immigration expansionist Linda Chavez, got him fired from *The Washington Times*. Indeed, even that first victim of what Murray Rothbard called "the neoconservative

Smearbund," Southern conservative literary scholar Mel Bradford, had a professional life after the neocons kept him from becoming Director of the National Endowment for the Humanities. Mel could and did return to a full professorship at the University of Dallas.

But Joe fell more catastrophically than the other neocon victims, from celebrity to almost total marginalization. In spite of all, he continued to put out newsletters and even occasionally got invited to give talks, in return for modest compensation. Among those who helped Joe through these difficult times were Fran Griffin, Lew Rockwell, the traditionalist Catholic magazine *The Wanderer*, and a few other publications that paid him for his writing. It was often distressing to read Joe's essays online or in his printed newsletter, knowing that this magnificent writer was going largely unread in his lifetime, while imbeciles and intellectual pygmies were being featured in prestigious and heavily funded neoconservative and liberal publications. Such disproportion between earthly accomplishments and earthly reward is enough to make one believe that all justice lies in the afterlife.

All the same, Joe's fate did not have the consequence that the neoconservatives intended. Rather than serving as a warning of what might befall those who practice right-wing deviationism or take unauthorized positions, Joe's outrageous reduction to a pariah generated resistance to the bullies who had gone after him. The steepness of his fall and the pious forbearance with which he treated his enemies had the effect of pouring steel into the spine of the independent Right. Machiavelli taught that it is better to be feared than to be loved but the worst thing is to be despised. Those who persecuted Joe and those who were the beneficiaries of this persecution became loathed by those whom this example of vengeance was supposed to render fearful.

It is also telling that for the younger generation on the independent Right, Joe is a hero, in a way that most paleoconservatives are not. The young admire him for having fought back, not only against the American global democratic empire but against the neoconservative commissars of the present conservative movement. Joe didn't change the subject when he smelled danger and he didn't care how many members of the New York *nomenklatura* he offended by speaking his mind. He suffered grievously for his honesty, while others were making careers by truckling. Whatever his faults, they pale beside his luminous virtues. *Requiescat in pace Dei!*

24. GEORGE F. KENNAN'S REALISM

Society, Volume 47, Number 4, 2010

The death of George F. Kennan, at the age of 101, on March 17, 2005, was followed by two Kennan-biographies: a widely reviewed work by John Lukacs in 2007 and a less widely noted one by Lee Congdon a year later. These works may signal a new series of studies on the architect of post-war containment. But they are not the first examinations of a fascinating, multifaceted life. In 1989 Wilson D. Miscamble and three years later, Walter L. Hixson brought out books concentrating on Kennan as an isolated voice of opposition to the anti-Communist passions of the Cold War. It is important to note that these authors were writing at a time when the Soviet empire was crumbling. They saw this situation as confirming Kennan's view that once Communist Russia had been contained, it would eventually crumble through internal weaknesses.

Meanwhile John Lewis Gaddis, in his book on containment doctrine in 1982 and then in a study of Soviet-American relations in 1992, presents Kennan as a wise advocate of a cautious approach toward the Soviets after the Second World War. While Gaddis has not produced a full-length biography of Kennan, he has dealt in considerable detail with his diplomatic career, his authorship of "The Long Telegram from Moscow" sent to Secretary of State James Byrnes in 1946, and with his 1947 article "The Sources of Soviet Conduct." It would in fact be no exaggeration to say that Kennan's reputation as a foreign policy expert rests partly on Gaddis's picture of the man and his work.

Much of the rest of Kennan's reputation may be attributed to his two-volume set of memoirs, going from 1925 through 1963, and published between 1967 and 1972, and his many studies and lectures dealing with Russia, the concept of containment, and foreign policy realism. Kennan left behind a paper trail spanning more than seventy years. And whether the organizer of the Policy Planning Staff of the State Department, Ambassador to Russia and later, Yugoslavia, or an

153

honored member of the Princeton Institute for Advanced Studies after 1951, he wrote and lectured nonstop. Congdon's title, which underscores Kennan's preoccupation with the written word, is entirely appropriate. That is exactly the way his subject would have wanted to be remembered. In his conversations with his admirer John Lukacs, Kennan made no secret about the importance he placed on his decades of reflection and on his habit of recording his thoughts.

Although Kennan attracted followings from across the ideological spectrum, much of this following has come from those who read him selectively. It would not be an overstatement to note that Kennan's way of viewing the world no longer has the slightest appeal to our academic and journalistic elites. Much of what made him popular during the second half of his life was based on interpreting him through filtered lenses. Kennan was never the person he seemed to many of his most effusive fans. For example, Cold War revisionist John Kane in *Between Virtue and Power* deplores the apparent fact that Truman abandoned Kennan's "pragmatic views" in dealing with Stalin; "His [Truman's] was to be more a political and economic strategy than a purely military one. But events would drag Truman much farther than he had intended to go — or that Kennan had thought wise." And so Truman responded with "overblown rhetoric." In Truman Doctrine, the American president went beyond anything that Kane or presumably Kennan considered prudent: "it risked being seen by Stalin as a provocation and threat that might induce him to respond aggressively."

Curiously, Kane, who tries to be understanding toward Stalin (who killed even more people than Hitler) raises no objection when he quotes Wilson's Anglophile Secretary of State Edward Lansing on the "autocratic" and "militaristic" danger of the Central Powers. Why, however, was Stalin less of a threat to us than was the imperfect constitutional monarchy of Kaiser Wilhelm? That question, according to his biographer Lee Congdon, was one that preoccupied Kennan for many decades. Indeed Kennan, who deeply admired the German Second Empire and the founder of that empire, Otto von Bismarck, sent a memo to the State Department in 1945 suggesting the merits of a Hohenzollern restoration in Central Europe: "The only reasonably respectable tradition of humane and orderly government in Germany is actually that of a strong, monarchical government."

Congdon, Lukacs and Gaddis all show that despite his rhetorical reservations about the neo-Wilsonian tone of Truman's declared support for the Greek government against Communist insurgents, Kennan endorsed Truman's policy — and the subsequent Marshall Plan. Gaddis details then Secretary of State George Marshall's close working relation to Kennan, who assisted the state department in helping to draft the Marshall Plan. Even more illuminating is a key paragraph from the Long Telegram to Byrnes in 1946, one that underscores Kennan's suspicion of world Communism. According to Congdon, this expression of concern was not unusual in Kennan's writings of the 1930s and 1940s, seeing that he had feared and loathed Communism even more than fascism:

> "Inner central core of Communist parties in other countries. While many of the persons who compose this category may also appear and act in unrelated public capacities, they are in reality working closely together as an underground operating directorate of world communism, a concealed Comintern tightly coordinated and directed by Moscow. It is important to remember that this inner core is actually working on underground lines, despite legality of parties with which it is associated."

Congdon's citations indicate that Kennan's view of Communism had more in common with that of the anti-Soviet American Right than is ordinarily thought to be the case. One should not confuse Kennan's misgivings about a third "democratic crusade" being launched against an American enemy during his lifetime with a "revisionist" view of the Communists as mere "radical democrats." His works abound in grim invectives against the Left's "utopian projects" and their totalitarian implications; and Congdon provides a chrestomathy of such passages, although after the 1960s they became fewer than those that had appeared before the Second World War.

But there is also considerable evidence for a different Kennan persona, one that seems less characteristic of the anti-Communist Right. According to Gaddis, "Kennan did not see the ideological writings of Marx and Lenin as a reliable guide with which to anticipate Soviet behavior. Ideology was not so much a guide to action as a justification for actions already decided on." At times Kennan went so far in denying the ideological aspect of Soviet Marxism that one finds this in his memoirs from October 1946: "I think it is a mistake that the Soviet leaders wish to establish a Communist form of government in the ring of states surrounding the Soviet Union on the west and the south. What they wish to do is to establish in those states governments amenable to their own influence and authority. The main thing is that these governments should follow Moscow's leadership."

The question here is not whether Kennan's understanding of Stalin's intentions was correct. Even at the time he was writing his relevant opinion, the Soviets were going after non-Communist parties in Poland, Hungary, Rumania, and elsewhere in their empire. Soon after they'd be imposing on their satellites the disastrous agricultural collectivism Stalin had already inflicted on the Soviet Union, at the cost of millions of deaths. But at issue here is not whether Kennan was correct in his judgment about Eastern Europe or whether he said things about Soviet intentions that later revisionist historians of the Cold War would be able to use. (The answer to the first question is no and the answer to the second is yes.) What his post-war writings seem to suggest is something more directly related to our purposes, namely, that Kennan's anti-anti-Communist interpreters do not have to invent texts in order to find evidence for their interpretation.

John Lukacs praises the "realism" that Kennan displayed in rejecting the anti-Communist ideology of the 1950s. He contrasts him to the Cold Warriors in the Eisenhower administration, and particularly to the ideologically anti-Communist Secretary of State John Foster Dulles. Lukacs also cites contemptuous remarks that Kennan directed at Ronald Reagan, as the instigator of heightened tensions with the Soviets. The reviewer of his book in *The New York Times* (April 29, 2007), James Traub, implies that Lukacs plays off the good Kennan against the bad George W. Bush, who "sought to pursue a policy of democracy promotion, spreading American virtues around the globe." Kennan's chief practical virtue for Lukacs was his opposition to the anti-Communist fervor of the Cold War, seen in his insistence that Communist powers were often nationalist regimes, with limited geopolitical ambitions. From his remarks on this subject, it seems that Lukacs regards Hitler to have been a far worse nationalist threat than his onetime ally in aggression Stalin. What is less clear is that Kennan made the same judgment as his longtime admirer, friend and biographer.

But Lukacs is definitely on target when he identifies his subject's view of the atmosphere of the early Cold War with a speech that Kennan delivered at the University of Notre Dame in May 1953, one that contains this key passage: Rabid anti-Communists "impel us in the name of our salvation from the dangers of Communism — to many of the habits of thought and action which our Soviet adversaries, I am sure, would like to see us adopt. I have lived more than 10 years of my life in totalitarian countries. I know where this sort of thing leads." Here too, however, there is need for a wider perspective. One should not present Kennan's expressions of opposition to American crusading excesses in 1953, as being exclusively directed against Republican anti-Communists or McCarthyism. (To his credit, Lukacs does not make such an assumption.) During the war Kennan had uttered even more passionate objections against rampant Teutonophobia, the aerial bombing of civilian populations in Central Europe, and the transformation of a struggle to remove the Nazi government in Germany into a world crusade. Unlike his selective admirers, Kennan was perfectly consistent, as Congdon points out, in his dislike for American crusades against "anti-democratic foes."

Still one can find passages by Kennan written during the Cold War which might have come from someone on the left. The Reith Lectures, which he presented at Oxford in 1957, offer such illustrative material. In these lectures, which drew favorable comments from his colleagues at the Princeton Institute for Advanced Studies, but anger from the Cold War liberal *Reporter*, Kennan took what might have been viewed as leftist positions in the 1950s. He advocated the neutralization of central Europe, in accordance with a plan that the Soviets had previously been floating for a neutralized Germany, assigning more diplomatic importance to the UN, and focusing on American social problems rather than on further confrontations with the Soviets. In these lectures we find the memorable lines: "To my own countrymen who had often asked me where best to apply the hand to counter the Soviet threat, I have had to reply: to our American failings — to the things that we are ashamed of in our own eyes: to the racial problems, to the conditions in our big cities, to the education and environment of our young people, to the growing gap between specialized knowledge and popular understanding."

Such quotations, nonetheless, do not invalidate other, perhaps more numerous passages from Kennan's work that reveal a different side of his thinking. In his *New York Times* review, Traub points to Lukacs's apparent uneasiness in having to explain the now unfashionable stands that Kennan had taken before the Second World War.

In the 1930s he had advocated "for America a more authoritarian model of government in which both immigration and suffrage would be curtailed." Moreover, Kennan "could not bring himself to despise Germany before, during or after the war," and he had opposed giving American protection to those who were escaping the Nazis after Hitler had marched into Prague. In partial defense of this last and most controversial position, Congdon and Lukacs both note that in 1939 Kennan did not want to draw the U.S. into another European war, especially without due provocation.

Traub's perception of a Kennan who did not quite fit in with his liberal admirers is correct. Moreover, Congdon and (to a lesser extent) Lukacs leave no doubt that their subject was a man of the Right, and particularly during the first half of his life. Unlike his nineteenth-century cousin and namesake, a Siberian explorer and patron of Russian anarchists, the second George Kennan was never at home on the left. Congdon quotes Kennan about the achievements of Austrian clerical fascism and about the austere honesty of the Portuguese authoritarian conservative Antonio Salazar. He also cites his many nostalgic references to Wilhelmine Germany to prove that Kennan was indeed a strange favorite of the anti-anti-Communist Left, to whatever extent he became such during the second half of his life.

Congdon also furnishes evidence that Kennan clung to his self-consciously anti-democratic, pro-aristocratic opinions well into the Cold War era. He alternated his warnings against the arms race and against the Vietnam War in *The New York Review of Books* with favorable references in the same publication to the Prussian aristocratic opponents of the Nazis. In his observations about Gottfried von Bismarck and Count Helmut von Moltke and other "Protestant Christian conservative" anti-Nazis, one finds definite traces of Kennan's pre-war political and cultural predilections. In *Russia and the West under Lenin and Stalin* (1961), Kennan has this to say to his readers: "I hold the First World War to be *the* great catastrophe of Western civilization in the present century." Then, after a denunciation of the Versailles Treaty, he lets it be known that "a German victory would not have been *quite* such a catastrophe." Despite his Germanophile feelings (which were certainly not shared by his anti-anti-Communist interpreters), Kennan nonetheless praises the tsarist regime that had fallen in February 1917. He emphatically preferred the Tsar to his Communist successor (and to the weak intervening Kerensky regime).

GEORGE F. KENNAN'S REALISM

Kennan likewise presents the view that the Soviets, even before the Nazis came along, had given birth to "the idea of the concentration camp system." Indeed "the true father of the Bolshevik concentration camps — was Lenin." In *Russia and the West*, it is possible to discern a later controversial thesis, presented by such diverse interpreters of modern European history as Ernst Nolte, Richard Pipes, and Paul Johnson, that Hitler was copying the Soviets when he created Nazi concentration camps. Kennan had put forth the same idea decades before, without forfeiting the good will of his politically correct readers.

Similar anti-Communist sentiments can be found in *American Diplomacy*, the book that came out of the Walgreen Lectures Kennan delivered at the University of Chicago in 1950. Here Kennan argues that "there was no adequate justification [in 1944] for refusing to give any attention to these developments [the opening of a second front against Nazi Germany] and for continuing a program of lavish and almost indiscriminate aid to the Soviet Union at a time when there was increasing reason to doubt whether her purposes in eastern Europe, aside from the defeat of Germany, would be ones which we Americans could approve and sponsor." In the same work, Kennan goes on to deplore "the mistake of unconditional surrender," and he typically dwells on the bravery of the conservative, aristocratic opponents of Hitler.

Congdon also quotes from a well-publicized interview that Kennan granted Hungarian journalist George Urban in 1976 and which subsequently was quoted at length in *Encounter*. Here Kennan attacked the modern fixation with equality and described human rights as something "remote from human authorship" and as giving rise to a "philosophical thicket where I cannot follow." In what became the most famous lines in this interview, Kennan sketched his reaction to the youth culture that he and his Norwegian wife had encountered upon sailing into a Danish port while on a Baltic cruise: "The place was swarming with hippies — motorbikes, girl-friends, drugs, pornography, drunkenness, noise — it was all there. I looked at this mob and thought how one company of robust infantry would drive it out of town."

Equally revealing were statements that Kennan made near the end of his life, about immigration and the cultural and political disorder that development had produced. In one especially candid interview with *The New Yorker* in 2000, he observed: "I think the country is coming apart partly because of its susceptibility to immigration." In his last full-length work *Around the Cragged Hill* (1993), he combines critical remarks about immigration with a call for dividing the U.S. into regions. Such a revamping seemed necessary in a society that no longer shared a cultural tradition and which was only held together by public administration and certain habits of consumption. Congdon also notes Kennan's ecological concerns, which caused him to champion Rachel Carson's attack in *The Silent Spring* on industrial and consumer waste. But Congdon does not read into this more than he has to. Kennan's ecological stand went along with his agrarianism and opposition to immigration. As in Europe until the last few decades, ecological interests were by no means restricted to the socialist Left.

Not surprisingly, Kennan has become a hated figure for those who celebrate American democracy and who advocate an American democratic mission to the world. In 1987, Cold War liberal Paul Hollander, mocked Kennan "as someone not concerned about inequalities. His main concern lies with standards: moral, cultural, aesthetic, or environmental." According to Hollander, "by Kennan's criteria, one is unable to censure South African whites who repress and murder blacks, because they feel threatened by the prospect of revolution and loss of power." Hollander also lambasts Kennan's negative view of contemporary America, which he associates with "violent crime, pornography, drug abuse and family breakdown." More recently a European, self-identified neoconservative journalist Joseph Joffe has criticized Lukacs, in a review of his Kennan-biography in the *Wall Street Journal* (July 6, 2007), for not being sufficiently critical of Kennan's "baffling appreciation" of ultraconservative interwar leaders. From Joffe's standpoint, Kennan held the wrongheaded view that "their kind of authoritarian government was a healthy and welcome alternative to inefficient parliamentary democracy."

Significantly another neoconservative commentator on international affairs Robert Kagan in *The Return of History and the End of Dreams* has omitted Kennan from his list of model guides for a moderate realist foreign policy for the U.S. For Kagan, the realist teachers whom he would like us to follow are Hans Morgenthau and Reinhold Niebuhr, both men of the democratic Left who had cautioned against excessive zeal during the Cold War. Although Hollander does not prove that Kennan admired the apartheid government of South Africa, it is true that Kennan feared revolutionary change more than he disliked the policy of racial separation. But still one wonders whether Hollander might express the same blanket condemnation of Afrikaner rule in view of the growing violence and white flight that have spread over post-apartheid South Africa. As for the judgment, however, that Kennan was essentially a man of the Right, it seems that Hollander was correct in this assessment.

Kennan's removal as ambassador to Russia did not result from the fact that he was less anti-Soviet than the "hawkish" John Foster Dulles, as Eisenhower's Secretary of State is described in Wikipedia. Kennan began speaking ill of Dulles, after the Eisenhower administration had failed to renew his ambassadorship to Russia, a position that he had received from President Truman in May 1952. By then, however, Kennan had said very indiscreet things in an interview given to reporters at the Berlin airport *en route* to a conference in London. When asked about his treatment in Moscow, he had lashed out at the government of Stalin for having turned ambassadors into "internees" in what Kennan compared to a prison system.

This incident caused Kennan to be repeatedly mentioned in the Soviet press as a warmonger, a charge that had first been laid at his doorstep after Soviet intelligence had come up with the text of his Long Telegram to Secretary of State Byrnes. Dulles had sent Kennan packing to avoid an imbroglio with the Soviets. And the man who was named Kennan's successor, Charles E. Bohlen, was thought to be less confrontational in dealing with Stalin. Kennan's replacement casts doubt on a pet idea held by some on the left, that the Republican administration had removed Kennan for being insufficiently anti-Soviet.

Lukacs and Congdon (who are actually close friends) both insist that Kennan's worldview changed only minimally throughout his adult life. He was a social conservative and foreign-policy realist who despised Wilsonian idealism and who expressed deep distrust about democracy at home and abroad. These views are much in evidence in *Russia and the West*. There Kennan quotes the French aristocratic student of American democracy, Tocqueville, on the total unsuitability of democratic regimes for rational statecraft. According to Kennan and Tocqueville, "democracies have the most confused and erroneous ideas on external affairs," exhibiting a tendency to be carried away by idealistic rhetoric and then to be pulled back and forth by fluctuating factional governments.

Despite signs of continuity in his worldview, Kennan generally moved toward the left from the 1950s onward. His Reith Lectures (1957), as Congdon observes, caused even liberal opponents of the Soviets "to take him to task" for being indifferent toward Soviet aggressiveness. Furthermore, in his discussion of "internal decay" as the real American crisis, he emphasized such themes as racial inequality and industrial waste. By the 1950s Kennan was no longer visiting Salazar, Dollfuss, and Franco but was the esteemed colleague and friend of an atomic physicist declared to be a security risk, Robert Oppenheimer, at the Princeton Institute for Advanced Studies. Kennan's stated pre-war concern that blacks voting would drive the American regime leftward had been replaced, in the Reith Lectures, by a stress on the need for racial equality.

In his 1984 additions to *American Diplomacy*, Kennan evinces what might have seemed anachronistic hostility toward the "group of right-wing senators" in the China Lobby who had accused "Dean Acheson and the Democratic Party" of having "lost China." And the elderly Kennan came out with guns blazing at another favorite target of the Left: "the wave of anti-Communist hysteria which was soon to become known as McCarthyism — an episode in our public life so disgraceful that one blushes to think about it." Why was such anger being vented at a chronologically distant unpleasantness, one that had been overshadowed by other evils in Kennan's intervening discourse, for example, student radicalism, the rising tide of political correctness, and environmental blight? Although Kennan had never been well-disposed toward the junior senator from Wisconsin, one might wonder at the public anger that was being directed at McCarthy and by implication, the 1950s decades later. This, by the way, came at a time when such hard leftists as Lillian Hellman and Ellen Schrecker were gaining favorable attention with their jeremiads against the "scoundrel times" and "witch hunts" of the 1950s.

A bit of contextualization might be in order here. What was happening during the last several decades of Kennan's life might have forced him and other, like-minded thinkers into a modification of their views along certain lines. Like other pre-World War Two traditionalists, Kennan had to preserve his credibility in the leftward moving political and cultural climate that has characterized the U.S. and other Western societies after the Second World War, and particularly from the 1960s onward. If Kennan had been born a half century later, it is probable that he would have been considered excessively right-wing and would not have risen to become a respected public figure. Nor would *The New Yorker* as late as 2000 have bothered to interview him and print what for its editors must have been unsettlingly reactionary opinions about immigration and social *mores*. Far more likely a much younger and less esteemed Kennan would have been held up to ridicule by pro-immigration lobbyists. It was Kennan's good fortune to have been born exactly when he was and to have been able to establish himself as an author and diplomat before 1945.

At the same time, like other traditionalists in Europe, such as Martin Heidegger, Arnold Gehlen, and Carl Schmitt, Kennan might have felt pushed in his later years to assume a certain protective coloration. This type of coloration, expressed as ecological complaints and laments about American zeal in the Cold War, was not necessarily assumed in a dishonest way; rather these stands were exaggerated for effect.

One of those who welcomed the Reith Lectures and congratulated Kennan for having given them was his companion at the Princeton Institute Ernst Kantorowicz (1895-1963). A German Jewish refugee who went to Berkeley in 1939 by way of England, Kantorowicz was known in the post-war years for his Anglophone study of medieval monarchy, *The King's Two Bodies* (1957). Kantorowicz increased his visibility by the vehement way in which he reacted to post-war American anti-Communism. He became Kennan's colleague at the Princeton Institute, after having refused to take an anti-Communist loyalty oath in California. And it would appear from his comments on the Reith Lectures, to which Congdon refers, that Kantorowicz had adapted well to the left-of-center environment at the Institute and to colleagues such as Oppenheimer.

Remarkably enough, Kantorowicz had been a hero of the German intellectual Right in a previous incarnation. His hagiographic and German nationalist biography of Holy Roman Emperor Frederick II (first published in 1927) had been acclaimed by German conservatives, even though its author was Jewish. Nothing in Kantorowicz's background, before he emerged as an anti-anti-Communist in the 1950s, would suggest that he had had the slightest sympathy for the Left. Into the 1950s he continued to speak about his honorable service in the German *Freikorps* and about how as a member of that German paramilitary group, he had helped put down the Spartacist uprising in Berlin in 1919.

But it could not have hurt Kantorowicz's reputation in a changing world to be seen as a victim of McCarthyism, any more than it hurt the reputations of certain Central Europeans of the Right to blame the U.S. for bad relations with the Soviets or to castigate Americans for the continued division of Germany. (In fact it was the American government and the pro-American Adenauer government in Germany that spurned Soviet overtures for a neutralized but unified Germany.)

Kennan, a traditionalist and one attracted to Central European culture, seems to have taken a similar path. He was able to buy the good will of the Left by following (or appearing to follow) it on certain issues, while going his own way on other matters. (Lukacs makes this clear in his biography.) But once the Cold War had become past history, the very issue that allowed Kennan's Right to remain relevant and inoffensive ceased to matter. By then the anti-anti-Communist Left had given way to a radical cultural Left, and it is one that is still with us and which determines political acceptability. In the new political culture those burdened with Kennan's sensibilities are no longer able to find a place in the public conversation. They are routinely, for better or worse, dismissed as xenophobes or even "fascists." Their unseasonable thoughts are no longer welcome, even if they had once complained about the Cold War and industrial waste. If this is indeed the case, then Kennan was fortunate to have lived in the century he did.

25. INSTITUTIONS OF HIGHER EMOTING

Taki's Magazine, 25 July 2012

Recently I commented on a blunder by Pennsylvania Governor Tom Corbett, who suddenly wimped out after having proposed cutting 20 to 30 percent out of the state's allocation for "higher education." Corbett had a chance to do good by making our state universities cough up more of their own funding.

In constant dollars, our state and onetime private "institutions of higher learning" charge nearly four times more than what my parents and I paid for my college education in the early 1960s. There are multiple reasons for these swollen costs. One is the availability of government loans, which allow colleges to raise tuitions astronomically. Another is the demand that young people acquire a BA before they can secure employment. Administrative layers have also been piled on universities since the 1960s, sometimes mandated by the government to fight alleged discrimination against designated minorities. All these subinfeudated deanships cost megabucks, which naturally get passed on to the consumers.

Adding to the tab is the Club Med flavor of modern college life, which now entails Jacuzzi baths, high-definition TVs in every building, and exercise machines galore. Dining in these resorts is no longer an austere, monastic experience. Collegiate eating areas offer a wide variety of culinary choices, including lots of junk food to please the adolescent palate.

Colleges work hard to devise "new forms of learning" to make themselves competitive as "educational institutions." The kids are customers rather than novices at the temple of learning, while the faculty members are glorified resort facilitators. At most colleges, particularly those that are tuition-driven, mountains get moved to accommodate the kids. At the same time, colleges wish to make their activities at least *appear* to be educational.

There are other complicating factors. Most people, according to Charles Murray and other serious researchers, do not have enough intelligence to perform at a true college level. Learning foreign languages, studying theoretical science, doing mathematical equations, and engaging in abstract reasoning are not everyone's bag because only a minority of our population has the necessary cognitive gifts.

But those who are not cognitively qualified or who manifest no interest in books still *want* to go to college, and they can usually obtain the requisite funds to fulfill their wish. How then do you keep these customers happy once they arrive?

One method is the promotion of "hands-on learning," a form of "learning experience" that spares the customer the inconvenience of ever having to open up a book except to remove the cellophane wrapper. I have heard students say they picked a certain college because it did not oblige them to do "any book stuff." Instead they dive headfirst into "service learning." Whatever these buzzwords mean — whether picketing with the teachers' union at a state rally or emptying garbage cans in a Third World country — the students will not be forced to do "book stuff." For these kids there exists only "real learning."

"Distance learning" is another new "teaching delivery resource." The customers don't have to pull their wasted bodies out of bed in the morning to attend class but can complete college work on a computer in between playing video games.

Even better is the "semester abroad," which in my experience allows the students to receive college credit for transferring their dissipation and idling to a foreign country for six months. Usually the educational requirements are sufficiently flexible so as not to burden the tourists with undue learning while outside the U.S.

Another means of keeping intellectually unqualified students busy in a "learning environment" is the emphasis on "diversity." Entire majors and minors have sprung up around this expanding form of distance learning. One is taught to express endless sympathy for women, Third World peoples, alternative-lifestyle practitioners, and visible minorities who have allegedly been crushed by Western Christian Civilization's heterosexual white bigotry. One is also encouraged to decorate one's dorm door and even body with appropriate political testimonies and to express remorse or indignation over the stifling oppression in which one is forced to languish.

The best part is that one never has to study African or Asian languages or do anything that is intellectually taxing. One becomes educated merely by emoting — and of course by paying outrageous tuitions.

Other books published by Arktos:

Beyond Human Rights
by Alain de Benoist

Manifesto for a European Renaissance
by Alain de Benoist & Charles Champetier

The Problem of Democracy
by Alain de Benoist

Germany's Third Empire
by Arthur Moeller van den Bruck

The Arctic Home in the Vedas
by Bal Gangadhar Tilak

Revolution from Above
by Kerry Bolton

The Fourth Political Theory
by Alexander Dugin

Metaphysics of War
by Julius Evola

The Path of Cinnabar:
An Intellectual Autobiography
by Julius Evola

Archeofuturism
by Guillaume Faye

Convergence of Catastrophes
by Guillaume Faye

Why We Fight
by Guillaume Faye

The WASP Question
by Andrew Fraser

The Saga of the Aryan Race volumes 1-2
by Porus Homi Havewala

The Saga of the Aryan Race volumes 3-5
by Porus Homi Havewala

The Owls of Afrasiab
by Lars Holger Holm

De Naturae Natura
by Alexander Jacob

Fighting for the Essence
by Pierre Krebs

Can Life Prevail?
by Pentti Linkola

A Handbook of Traditional Living
by Raido

The Agni and the Ecstasy
by Steven J. Rosen

The Jedi in the Lotus:
Star Wars and the Hindu Tradition
by Steven J. Rosen

It Cannot Be Stormed
by Ernst von Salomon

Tradition & Revolution
by Troy Southgate

Against Democracy and Equality
by Tomislav Sunic

The Initiate: Journal of Traditional Studies
by David J. Wingfield (ed.)

CPSIA information can be obtained at www.ICGtesting.com
Printed in the USA
BVOW03s1218131113

336199BV00001B/193/P